New Charter for Health Care Workers

Pontifical Council for Pastoral Assistance to Health Care Workers

Translated by
The National Catholic Bioethics Center

THE NATIONAL CATHOLIC BIOETHICS CENTER
Philadelphia

Contents

Preface

The Church has always considered serving the sick "an integral part of her mission,"[1] combining "the preaching of the Good News with the help and care of the sick."[2]

The vast world of service in response to human suffering "concerns the good of the human person and of society" itself.[3] For this very reason it also poses delicate and unavoidable questions, which involve not only a social and organizational aspect but also a uniquely ethical and religious one. This is because fundamental "human" events are implicated, such as suffering, sickness, and death, together with the related questions about the role of medicine and the mission of physicians with respect to sick persons.[4]

Pope St. John Paul II, as an interpreter of this command, founded the Pontifical Council for Pastoral Assistance to Health Care Workers on February 11, 1985. Inspired by faith and hope, he intended to offer a response to the challenges arising in the world of health care, appreciative of the task that many Christians—health care workers, lay persons, whether individually or in associations, consecrated men and women, priests and deacons—generously perform, bearing witness to the evangelical values of the dignity of the human person and respect for life through their closeness to the sick as well as through their work, study, and research.

In 1994, the first president of the dicastery, the late Fiorenzo Cardinal Angelini, published the *Charter for Health Care Workers*. It served as an effective tool for the initial and ongoing formation of those of various professions who work in the world of health care, and was eventually translated into nineteen languages.

Following upon new advances in the scientific and biomedical field since 1994 as well as magisterial pronouncements during the pontificates of Popes St. John Paul II, Benedict XVI, and Francis, the dicastery considered

---

1 John Paul II, Motu Proprio *Dolentium hominum* (February 11, 1985), n. 1: *AAS* 77 (1985), 457.

2 Ibid.

3 Ibid., n. 3.

4 Ibid.

it necessary to revise and update this document while keeping its original structure, focused on the calling of health care workers to be ministers of life.

The document now being published was updated and revised in more accessible, contemporary language. The methodology and structure were carefully checked, the theological notes of ecclesiastical documents cited were reviewed, and finally the content was updated.

In particular, I think it is necessary to point out that the *New Charter* addresses not only advances in the medical sciences and their possible repercussions on human life, but also legal questions, which increasingly affect and influence the exercise of the health care professions; it also addresses problems that are assuming greater importance, especially with regard to justice, as well as respect for and increased sensitivity to the principles of solidarity and subsidiarity in access to available pharmaceuticals and technologies. This is pertinent to the demands of social justice in the field of health care, inspired by the right to the preservation and promotion of health through fair health care policies.

It also takes into account an expansion of the personnel involved in this task, so that, besides the traditional health care professionals (physicians, nurses, and aides), others in the world of health care are included: biologists, pharmacists, health care workers in the field, administrators, and legislators in health care matters as well as workers in the public and private sectors who are involved in secular or faith-based initiatives.

This vocation, which has expanded in the number of positions, professional roles, and responsibilities in health care, is marked by the anthropological value that the biomedical sciences must promote amid the contemporary cultural trends as well, in their continual search to offer a specific service to the integral good of the life and dignity of every human being and in a fruitful dialogue between biomedicine and the moral principles found in the magisterium of the Church. This commitment is made by the Church itself with this *New Charter for Health Care Workers*, which is meant to be an effective tool for confronting the weakening of ethical standards and the subjectivity of consciences which, together with cultural, ethical, and religious pluralism, easily lead to relativism and hence to the risk that we will no longer be able to refer to a shared *ethos*, especially with regard to the major existential questions pertaining to the meaning of birth, life, and death.

The Charter certainly cannot amount to an exhaustive treatment of all the problems and questions that come up in the field of health care and sickness, but it was produced to offer the clearest possible guidelines for the ethical problems that must be addressed in the world of health care in general, in harmony with the teachings of Jesus Christ and the magisterium of the Church.

On the thirty-first anniversary of the institution of the Pontifical Council for Pastoral Assistance to Health Care Workers and the vigil of the twenty-fifth World Day of the Sick, I commend to the various lay and religious professionals who make up the complex world of health care this *New Charter for Health Care Workers*. It is my hope that this tool may contribute to an ongoing, profound renewal of the world of health care and of the Church's own pastoral activity in promoting and defending the dignity of the human person, helping to rewrite on a daily basis the parable of the Good Samaritan (cf. Lk 10:29–37) and to make present, even at moments of suffering and pain, Hope, the gift of Christ's Paschal mystery.

†ZYGMUNT ZIMOWSKI
President of the Pontifical Council
for Pastoral Assistance to
Health Care Workers

Abbreviations

AAS   *Acta apostolicae sedis*

CCC   *Catechism of the Catholic Church*

CIC   Code of Canon Law (1983)

INTRODUCTION

MINISTERS OF LIFE

1.   The activity of health care workers is basically a service to life and health, which are primary goods of the human person. To this service is dedicated the professional or volunteer activity of those who are involved in various ways in preventive medicine, treatment, and rehabilitation: physicians, pharmacists, nurses, technicians, hospital chaplains, men and women religious, administrative personnel, those who are responsible for national and international policies, and volunteers. "Their profession calls for them to be guardians and servants of human life,"[1] or indeed of the person whose inviolable dignity and transcendent vocation are rooted in the depths of his very being.[2] This dignity, which all human beings can recognize by reason, is elevated to a further level of life, that of God's own life, inasmuch as the Son, in becoming one of us, makes it possible for human beings to become "children of God" (Jn 1:12), "partakers of the divine nature" (2 Pet 1:4).

A service to life and health

In light of these tenets of the faith, the respect for the human person that human reason already demands is further accentuated and reinforced. "The different ways in which God, acting in history, cares for the world and for mankind are not mutually exclusive; on the contrary, they support each other and intersect. They have their origin and goal in the eternal, wise, and loving counsel whereby God predestines men and women 'to be conformed to the image of his Son' (Rom 8:29)."[3] "By taking the interrelationship of these two dimensions, *the human and the divine,* as the starting point, one understands better why it is that man has unassailable value: *he possesses an eternal vocation* and *is called to share in the trinitarian love of the living God.*"[4]

Human and divine nature

---

1   John Paul II, Encyclical Letter *Evangelium vitae,* On the Value and Inviolability of Human Life (March 25, 1995), n. 89: *AAS* 87 (1995), 502.

2   Cf. Congregation for the Doctrine of the Faith, Instruction *Dignitas personae,* On Certain Bioethical Questions (September 8, 2008), n. 5: *AAS* 100 (2008), 861.

3   Ibid., n. 7: *AAS* 100 (2008), 863.

4   Ibid., n. 8: *AAS* 100 (2008), 863.

2.   The activity of health care workers, in their complementary roles and responsibilities, has the value of service to the human person, since to protect, recover, and improve physical, psychological, and spiritual health means to serve life in its totality.[5]

A service to human fragility

Moreover, "in the current multifaceted philosophical and scientific context, a considerable number of scientists and philosophers, in the spirit of the Hippocratic Oath, see in medical science a service to human fragility aimed at the cure of disease, the relief of suffering and the equitable extension of necessary care to all people."[6]

"Therefore, it is easy to understand the importance, in the social health care services, of the presence ... of workers who are led by an integrally human view of illness and who as a result are able to effect a fully human approach to the sick person who is suffering."[7]

Health care and social health care

3.   Health care and social health care services are closely related. By the expression "health care" we mean everything pertaining to prevention, diagnosis, treatment, and rehabilitation for the better physical, psychological, social, and spiritual balance and well-being of the person. By the expression "social health care services" is meant anything concerned with health care policy, legislation, programs, and facilities.

It must be emphasized, nevertheless, that although institutions that provide these services are very important, no institution can by itself replace the human heart or human compassion when it is a matter of encountering the sufferings of another.[8]

---

5 Cf. John Paul II, Encyclical Letter *Evangelium vitae*, n. 89: *AAS* 87 (1995), 502.

6 Congregation for the Doctrine of the Faith, Instruction *Dignitas personae*, n. 2: *AAS* 100 (2008), 859.

7 John Paul II, Motu Proprio *Dolentium hominum* (February 11, 1985), n. 2: *AAS* 77 (1985), 458.

8 Cf. John Paul II, Apostolic Letter *Salvifici doloris*, On the Christian Meaning of Human Suffering (February 11, 1984), n. 29: *AAS* 76

4.   Health care is carried out in everyday practice in an interpersonal relationship characterized by the trust of a person who is experiencing suffering and sickness, who has recourse to the knowledge and conscience of a health care worker who encounters him in order to support and care for him, thus adopting a sincere attitude of "compassion," in the etymological sense of the word.[9]

Interpersonal relationship characterized by trust in conscience

Such a relationship with the sick person, with full respect for his autonomy, requires availability, attention, understanding, empathy, and dialogue, together with expertise, competence, and professional ethics. That is to say, it must be the expression of a profoundly human commitment, made and carried out not just as a technical activity but as an act of dedication and love of neighbor.

5.   Service to life is performed only in *fidelity to the moral law*, which expresses its value and duties. Indeed, for the health care worker there are moral responsibilities too, the guidelines for which spring from bioethical reflection. In this field, with vigilant, zealous attention, the magisterium of the Church makes pronouncements in reference to the questions raised by biomedical progress and by the changeable cultural *ethos*.

Fidelity to the moral norm

For the health care worker, this magisterium is a source of principles and norms of behavior, which enlightens his conscience and orients it—especially in the complexity of today's biotechnological possibilities—toward decisions that always respect the human person and his dignity. Through fidelity to the moral norm, the health care worker lives out his fidelity to man, whose

(1984), 244–246. "In the exercise of your profession, in fact, you are constantly dealing with the human person, who entrusts his body into your hands, trusting in your competence as well as in your solicitude and care. You deal with the mysterious and great reality of the life of a human being, with his suffering and his hope." (John Paul II, Address to the participants in a conference of surgeons [February 19, 1987], n. 2: *Insegnamenti* X/1 [1987], 374).

9   Cf. Benedict XVI, Encyclical Letter *Spe salvi*, On Christian Hope (November 30, 2007), n. 39: *AAS* 99 (2007), 1017.

value the norm safeguards, and to God, whose wisdom the norm expresses.

Advances in medicine and the constant appearance of new moral questions, therefore, require on the part of the health care worker a serious *preparation and ongoing formation* in order to maintain the necessary professional competence. To this end it is desirable that all health care workers be suitably trained and that those responsible for their professional formation endeavor to establish professorial chairs and courses in bioethics. Furthermore, in the principal hospital centers, the establishment of ethics committees for medical practice and clinical ethics services should be promoted. In them medical competence and evaluation meet and are integrated with the competence of other professionals who are attending the sick person, to safeguard the dignity of the patient and medical responsibility itself.[10]

Integral vision of the human person

6. The Church, in proposing moral principles and evaluations for biomedical science, *draws on the light of both reason and faith*, developing an integral vision of the human person and his vocation that is capable of accepting everything good that emerges from human works and from various cultural and religious traditions, which not infrequently show a great reverence for life.[11]

---

10 "It would on the one hand be illusory to claim that scientific research and its applications are morally neutral; on the other hand, one cannot derive criteria for guidance from mere technical efficiency, from research's possible usefulness to some at the expense of others or, worse still, from prevailing ideologies. Thus science and technology require, for their own intrinsic meaning, an unconditional respect for the fundamental criteria of the moral law: that is to say, they must be at the service of the human person, of his inalienable rights and his true and integral good according to the design and will of God" (Congregation for the Doctrine of the Faith, Instruction *Donum vitae*, On the Respect for Nascent Life and the Dignity of Procreation [February 22, 1987], n. 2: *AAS* 80 [1988], 73). Cf. *Catechism of the Catholic Church* (*CCC*), n. 2294.

11 "Especially significant is the reawakening of an ethical reflection on issues affecting life. The emergence and ever more widespread

The magisterium means to offer a word of support and encouragement for the perspective on culture that considers *science an invaluable service to the integral good of the life and dignity of every human being.* The Church, therefore, views scientific research with hope, and desires that many Christians will dedicate themselves to the progress of biomedicine and in this field will bear witness to their own faith.[12]

In particular, "the Church, by expressing an ethical judgment on some developments of recent medical research concerning man, ... does not intervene in the area proper to medical science itself, but rather calls everyone to ethical and social responsibility for their actions. She reminds them that the ethical value of biomedical science is gauged in reference to ... the *unconditional respect owed to every human being* at every moment of his or her existence."[13]

Ethical and social responsibility

It becomes clear therefore that "the intervention of the magisterium falls within its mission of *contributing to the formation of conscience,* by authentically teaching the truth that is Christ and at the same time by declaring and confirming authoritatively the principles of the moral order that spring from human nature itself."[14] This is also motivated by the fact that health care workers cannot be left alone and burdened by unbearable responsibilities when confronted with ever more complex and problematic clinical cases, which are made so by the biotechnological possibilities, many of them still in the experimental phase,

Formation of conscience

development of bioethics is promoting more reflection and dialogue—between believers and nonbelievers as well as between followers of different religions—on ethical problems, including fundamental issues pertaining to human life" (John Paul II, Encyclical Letter *Evangelium vitae,* n. 27: *AAS* 87 [1995], 432).

12   Cf. Congregation for the Doctrine of the Faith, Instruction *Dignitas personae,* n. 3: *AAS* 100 (2008), 860.

13   Ibid., n. 10: *AAS* 100 (2008), 864.

14   Ibid.: *AAS* 100 (2008), 865.

that are available to medicine today, and by the social–health care relevance of particular questions.[15]

Health care policy

7.   Those who are involved in health care policy and financial administrators have a responsibility not only to their specific fields, but also toward society and the sick.

It is up to them, in particular, to defend and promote the common good, performing the duty of justice,[16] according to the principles of solidarity and subsidiarity, in developing national and worldwide policies aimed at the authentic development of peoples, especially in the allocation of financial resources in the health care field.[17]

In this light, those responsible for health care policies can bring about fruitful collaboration by acknowledging the distinctive character of Catholic health care facilities, thereby contributing to the building of "the 'civilization of love and life,' without which the life of individuals and of society itself loses its most genuinely human quality."[18]

15   "The development of science and technology, this splendid testimony of the human capacity for understanding and for perseverance, does not free humanity from the obligation to ask the ultimate religious questions. Rather, it spurs us on to face the most painful and decisive of struggles, those of the heart and of the moral conscience" (John Paul II, Encyclical Letter *Veritatis splendor*, On Some Fundamental Questions about the Moral Teaching of the Church [August 6, 1993], n. 1: *AAS* 85 [1993], 1134).

16   "Its operative field is very vast: it goes from health education to the creation of greater sensitivity in those in public authority; from direct involvement in one's own workplace to forms of cooperation—local, national and international—which are made possible by the existence of so many organizations and associations which have among their purposes the call, direct or indirect, for a need to make medicine ever more human" (John Paul II, Address to participants in the conference sponsored by the Pontifical Commission for Pastoral Assistance to Health Care Workers [November 12, 1987], n. 6: *AAS* 80 [1988], 645).

17   Cf. Benedict XVI, Encyclical Letter *Caritas in veritate*, On Integral Human Development in Charity and Truth (June 29, 2009), nn. 38–39: *AAS* 101 (2009), 673–674.

18   John Paul II, Encyclical Letter *Evangelium vitae*, n. 27: *AAS* 87 (1995), 431.

8.   Animated by the Christian spirit and outlook, the *Profession,* health care worker discovers the transcendent dimension *mission, and* peculiar to his profession in its everyday practice. In fact, it *vocation* surpasses the purely human level of service to the suffering person and takes on the character of Christian witness, and therefore of mission.

Mission is equivalent to vocation;[19] that is, it is a response to a transcendent call that takes shape in the suffering face of the other. This activity is the prolongation and the fulfillment of the charity of Christ, who "went about doing good and healing all" (Acts 10:38).[20] At the same time it is charity directed toward Christ himself: He is the patient—"I was sick"—and so He considers care given to a brother as being rendered to himself: "You did it to me" (cf. Mt 25:31–40).[21] The health care worker is a reflection of the Good Samaritan in the parable, who stops for the injured man, becoming his "neighbor" in charity

---

19   "Your vocation is one which commits you to the noble mission of service to people in the vast, complex and mysterious field of suffering" (John Paul II, To representatives of the Italian Catholic Physicians [March 4, 1989], n. 2: *Insegnamenti* XII/1 [1989], 480).

20   "The very personal relationship of dialogue and trust which is established between you and the patient demands in you a charge of humanity which is resolved, for the believer, in the richness of Christian charity. It is this divine virtue which enriches your every action and gives to your acts, even the most simple ones, the power of an act performed by you in interior communion with Christ" (John Paul II, Address to the members of the Italian Dental Association [December 14, 1984], n. 4: *Insegnamenti* VII/2 [1984], 1594).

21   "Jesus, the evangelizer par excellence and the Gospel in person, identifies especially with the little ones (cf. Mt 25:40). This reminds us Christians that we are called to care for the vulnerable of the earth. But the current model, with its emphasis on success and self-reliance, does not appear to favor an investment in efforts to help the slow, the weak, or the less talented to find opportunities in life" (Francis, Apostolic Exhortation *Evangelii gaudium*, On the Proclamation of the Gospel in Today's World [November 24, 2013], n. 209: *AAS* 105 [2013], 1107).

(cf. Lk 10:29–37).[22] In this light, the health care worker can be considered a minister of God, who in Scripture is depicted as one "who love[s] the living" (Wis 11:26).

Participation in the pastoral activity of the Church

9.　　The Church considers "service to the sick and suffering as an integral part of her mission."[23] This means that the therapeutic ministry of health care workers participates in the pastoral and evangelizing activity of the Church.[24] Service to life thus becomes a ministry of salvation, or a proclamation that fulfills Christ's redeeming love.

22　Cf. John Paul II, Apostolic Letter *Salvifici doloris*, nn. 28–30: *AAS* 76 (1984), 242–246. "Allowing herself to be guided by the example of Jesus the 'Good Samaritan' (cf. Lk 10:29–37) and upheld by his strength, the Church has always been in the front line in providing charitable help: so many of her sons and daughters, especially men and women religious, in traditional and ever new forms, have consecrated and continue to consecrate their lives to God, freely giving of themselves out of love for their neighbor, especially for the weak and needy" (John Paul II, Encyclical Letter *Evangelium vitae*, n. 27: *AAS* 87 [1995], 431).

23　John Paul II, Motu Proprio *Dolentium hominum*, n. 1: *AAS* 77 (1985), 457. "A society truly welcomes life when it recognizes that it is also precious in old age, in disability, in serious illness and even when it is fading; when it teaches that the call to human fulfillment does not exclude suffering; indeed, when it teaches its members to see in the sick and suffering a gift for the entire community, a presence that summons them to solidarity and responsibility. This is the Gospel of life which, through your scientific and professional competence, and sustained by grace, you are called to spread" (Francis, Message to participants in the General Assembly of the Pontifical Academy for Life on the occasion of the twentieth anniversary of its founding [February 19, 2014]: *AAS* 106 [2014], 192).

24　"Your presence at the sickbed is bound up with that of those—priests, religious and laity—who are engaged in apostolate to the sick. Quite a number of the aspects of that apostolate coincide with the problems and tasks of the service to life rendered by medicine. There is a necessary interaction between the exercise of the medical profession and pastoral work, because the one object of both is the human person, seen in his dignity of a child of God, a brother or sister needing, just like ourselves, help and comforting" (John Paul II, Address to the World Congress of Catholic Physicians [October 3, 1982], n. 6: *Insegnamenti* V/3 [1982], 676).

"Just such people—doctors, nurses, other health care workers, volunteers—are called to be the living sign of Jesus Christ and his Church in showing love toward the sick and suffering,"[25] in other words, ministers of life.

10.   The present Charter wishes to support the *ethical fidelity of health care workers* in the decisions and the conduct in which their service to life is embodied. This fidelity is outlined according to the stages of human life: procreating, living, and dying, considered as important junctures for ethical and pastoral reflections.

Assurance of ethical fidelity

---

25   John Paul II, Apostolic Exhortation *Christifideles laici*, On the Vocation and Mission of Lay People in the Church and the World (December 30, 1988), n. 53: *AAS* 81 (1989), 500.

PROCREATING

11.   "In the biblical narrative, the difference between man and other creatures is shown above all by the fact that only the creation of man is presented as the result of a special decision on the part of God, a deliberation *to establish a particular and specific bond with the Creator:* 'Let us make man in our image, after our likeness' (Gen 1:26). *The life* which God offers to man *is a gift by which God shares something of himself with his creature.*"[26]

Value and dignity of human procreation

Human generation, therefore, cannot be compared with that of any other living being, because it is the generation of a person. Human life is the product of a gift, and it is transmitted through the gesture that expresses and incarnates love and the reciprocal self-giving of a man and a woman.

The very nature of procreation reveals that it must be understood and carried out according to the logic of the gift. The inseparable bond between conjugal love and human generation, imprinted on the nature of the human person, is a law by which everyone must be guided and to which everyone is held.[27]

12.   God himself "wished to share with man a certain special participation in his own creative work. Thus he blessed male and female saying, 'Increase and multiply' (Gen 1:28)."

Human procreation as a human and religious event

The generation of a new human being is therefore "an event which is deeply human and full of religious meaning, insofar as it involves both the spouses, who form 'one flesh' (Gen 2:24), and God who makes himself present."[28] The parents "actualize in history the original

26 John Paul II, Encyclical Letter *Evangelium vitae*, n. 34: *AAS* 87 (1995), 438–39.

27 Cf. Congregation for the Doctrine of the Faith, Instruction *Dignitas personae*, n. 6: *AAS* 100 (2008), 862.

28 John Paul II, Encyclical Letter *Evangelium vitae*, n. 43: *AAS* 87 (1995), 448.

blessing of the Creator—that of transmitting by procreation the divine image from person to person."[29]

At the service of responsible human procreation

13.   Health care workers fulfill their service in this very delicate area by helping parents to procreate responsibly, working to prevent and treat pathologies that interfere with fertility, while protecting sterile couples from an invasive and excessively technology-focused approach that is unworthy of human procreation.

Fertility regulation

Responsible procreation and cooperation with God

14.   "The true practice of conjugal love, and the whole meaning of the family life which results from it, have this aim: that the couple be ready with stout hearts to cooperate with the love of the Creator and the Savior, who through them will enlarge and enrich His own family day by day."[30] "When a new person is born of the conjugal union of the two, he brings with him into the world a particular image and likeness of God himself: *the genealogy of the person is inscribed in the very biology of generation.* In affirming that the spouses, as parents, cooperate with God the Creator in conceiving and giving birth to a new human being, we are not speaking merely with reference to the laws of biology. ... Begetting is the continuation of Creation."[31]

"Responsible parenthood is exercised by those who prudently and generously decide to have more children, and by those who, for serious reasons and with due respect to moral precepts, decide not to have additional children

---

29 John Paul II, Apostolic Exhortation *Familiaris consortio*, On the Duties of the Christian Family in Today's World (November 22, 1981), n. 28: *AAS* 74 (1982), 114. Cf. John Paul II, Letter *Gratissimam sane*, To Families (February 2, 1994), n. 9: *AAS* 86 (1994), 878.

30 Vatican Council II, Pastoral Constitution *Gaudium et spes* (December 7, 1965), n. 50. Cf. Paul VI, Encyclical Letter *Humanae vitae* (July 25, 1968), n. 9: *AAS* 60 (1968), 487.

31 John Paul II, Encyclical Letter *Evangelium vitae*, n. 43: *AAS* 87 (1995), 448.

for either a certain or an indefinite period of time."[32] This gives rise to the need for a way of regulating fertility that is an expression of conscious and responsible openness to the transmission of life.

15.   In evaluating actions with regard to this regulation, moral judgment "does not depend solely on sincere intentions or on an evaluation of motives, but must be determined by objective standards [which are] based on the nature of the human person and his acts."[33] This is a question of the dignity of the man and the woman and of their intimate relationship. Respect for this dignity characterizes the truth of conjugal love.

Standards for moral evaluation

As for the conjugal act, it expresses "the inseparable connection ... between the unitive significance and the procreative significance which are both inherent to the marriage act."[34] In fact, the acts with which the spouses fully realize and intensify their union are the same acts that generate life, and vice versa.[35]

Love that is expressed in the "language of the body" is at the same time unitive and procreative: it "clearly involves both 'spousal meanings' and parental ones."[36] This connection is intrinsic to the conjugal act: it cannot "be broken by man of his own initiative" without

Spousal and parental meanings

---

32   Paul VI, Encyclical Letter *Humanae vitae*, n. 10: *AAS* 60 (1968), 487.

33   Vatican Council II, Pastoral Constitution *Gaudium et spes*, n. 51.

34   Paul VI, Encyclical Letter *Humanae vitae*, n. 12: *AAS* 60 (1968), 488–489.

35   "The fundamental nature of the marriage act, while uniting husband and wife in the closest intimacy, also renders them capable of generating new life—and this as a result of laws written into the actual nature of man and of woman" (Paul VI, Encyclical Letter *Humanae vitae*, n. 12: *AAS* 60 [1968], 488–489).

36   Cf. Congregation for the Doctrine of the Faith, Instruction *Donum vitae*, II, B, 4b: *AAS* 80 (1988), 91.

denying the inherent dignity of the human person and "the inner truth of conjugal love."[37]

Natural methods

16.　　When there are justified, responsible reasons for spacing births, and therefore a couple needs to avoid conception,[38] it is licit for the couple to abstain from sexual relations in the fertile periods, which are identified through so-called natural methods of regulating fertility. On the other hand it is illicit to resort to contraception, that is, "any action which either before, at the moment of, or after sexual intercourse is specifically intended to prevent procreation—whether as an end or as a means."[39]

"When, instead, by means of recourse to periods of infertility, the couple respect the inseparable connection between the unitive and procreative meanings of human sexuality, they are acting as 'ministers' of God's plan and they 'benefit from' their sexuality according to the original dynamism of 'total' self-giving, without manipulation or alteration."[40] Such a way of living out human sexuality, by means of knowledge about the physiological rhythms of the woman's fertility and infertility, can help to bring about authentic, responsible procreation. The periodic recurrence of the fertile phase in the woman's cycle prompts the spouses to ask themselves from time to time about the

---

37　Paul VI, Encyclical Letter *Humanae vitae*, n. 12: *AAS* 60 (1968), 488; cf. John Paul II, Apostolic Exhortation *Familiaris consortio*, n. 32: *AAS* 74 (1982), 118. "Consequently, 'the man who wishes to understand himself thoroughly—and not just in accordance with immediate, partial, often superficial, and even illusory standards and measures of his being—must with his unrest, uncertainty and even his weakness and sinfulness, with his life and death, draw near to Christ'" (John Paul II, Encyclical Letter *Veritatis splendor*, n. 8: *AAS* 85 [1993], 1139).

38　Paul VI, Encyclical Letter *Humanae vitae*, n. 10: *AAS* 60 (1968), 487.

39　Ibid., n. 14: *AAS* 60 (1968), 490.

40　John Paul II, Apostolic Exhortation *Familiaris consortio*, n. 32: *AAS* 74 (1982), 119.

motives that lead them to openly seek out the generation of a child or to postpone that possibility.[41]

Contraceptive methods, in contrast, are "equally repugnant to the nature of man and of woman" and of their "intimate relationship."[42] In these cases, sexual union is intentionally cut off from procreation: the act is thwarted in its natural openness to life. "Thus the original import of human sexuality is distorted and falsified, and the two meanings, unitive and procreative, inherent in the very nature of the conjugal act, are artificially separated: in this way the marriage union is betrayed and its fruitfulness is subjected to the caprice of the couple."[43] In using contraceptive methods, the spouses "act as 'arbiters' of the divine plan and they 'manipulate' and degrade human sexuality—and with it themselves and their married partner—by altering its value of 'total' self-giving."[44]

Contraception

17.   The difference between recourse to natural methods and recourse to contraception for the spacing of births is not situated simply at the level of techniques or methods, in which the decisive element would be the artificial or the natural character of the procedure.[45] It is a question, rather, of a much more vast and profound difference which

Anthropological and moral difference between natural methods and contraception

---

41   "It is precisely this respect which makes legitimate, at the service of responsible procreation, *the use of natural methods of regulating fertility*. From the scientific point of view, these methods are becoming more and more accurate and make it possible in practice to make choices in harmony with moral values" (John Paul II, Encyclical Letter *Evangelium vitae*, n. 97: *AAS* 87 [1995], 512).

42   Paul VI, Encyclical Letter *Humanae vitae*, n. 13: *AAS* 60 (1968), 489.

43   John Paul II, Encyclical Letter *Evangelium vitae*, n. 23: *AAS* 87 (1995), 427.

44   John Paul II, Apostolic Exhortation *Familiaris consortio*, n. 32: *AAS* 74 (1982), 119.

45   "Natural" techniques aimed at preventing fertilization by means of an incomplete sexual act are in fact contraceptive.

by nature is "both anthropological and moral"[46] and in the final analysis involves "two irreconcilable concepts of the human person and of human sexuality."[47]

Unitive and procreative meanings of natural methods

18.   The natural methods correspond, therefore, to the meaning attributed to conjugal love, which directs and determines the couple's experience: "The choice of the natural rhythms involves accepting the cycle of the person—that is, the woman—and thereby accepting dialogue, reciprocal respect, shared responsibility, and self-control. To accept the cycle and to enter into dialogue means to recognize both the spiritual and corporal character of conjugal communion and to live personal love with its requirement of fidelity. In this context the couple comes to experience how conjugal communion is enriched with those values of tenderness and affection that constitute the inner soul of human sexuality, in its physical dimension also. In this way sexuality is respected and promoted in its truly and fully human dimension, and is never 'used' as an 'object' that, by breaking the personal unity of soul and body, strikes at God's creation itself at the level of the deepest interaction of nature and person."[48]

Abortion as an extension of contraception

19.   In order to justify the practice, "it is frequently asserted that contraception, if made safe and available to all, is the most effective remedy against abortion. ... When looked at carefully, this objection is clearly unfounded. ... Indeed, the pro-abortion culture is especially strong precisely where the Church's teaching on contraception is rejected."[49] No doubt contraception and abortion, from the moral perspective, are evils of different kinds but are

---

46   John Paul II, Apostolic Exhortation *Familiaris consortio*, n. 32: *AAS* 74 (1982), 120.

47   Ibid.

48   Ibid.

49   John Paul II, Encyclical Letter *Evangelium vitae*, n. 13: *AAS* 87 (1995), 414.

closely related "as fruits of the same tree."[50] Contraception uses all the means at its disposal to prevent a new life from coming into existence. If, despite the contraception, a new life is engendered, it is often rejected and aborted. Contraception, far from making abortion less common, finds therein its logical extension.

20.   In the area of contraception, one particularly important technique is contraceptive or anti-procreative sterilization,[51] which can be voluntary or compulsory.[52]

No to voluntary sterilization

In particular, voluntary sterilization, whether permanent or temporary, aimed directly at obtaining infertility, whether male or female, is always morally illicit and

---

50   Ibid.: *AAS* 87 (1995), 415.

51   Cf. Ibid., nn. 16–17: *AAS* 87 (1995), 418–419.

52   In summary form, the teaching of the Church is restated with reference to various forms of sterilization in these terms: "Any sterilization which of itself, that is, of its own nature and condition, has the sole immediate effect of rendering the generative faculty incapable of procreation, is to be considered direct sterilization, as the term is understood in the declarations of the pontifical magisterium, especially of Pius XII. Therefore, notwithstanding any subjectively right intention of those whose actions are prompted by the care or prevention of physical or mental illness which is foreseen or feared as a result of pregnancy, such sterilization remains absolutely forbidden according to the doctrine of the Church. And indeed the sterilization of the faculty itself is forbidden for an even graver reason than the sterilization of individual acts, since it induces a state of sterility in the person which is almost always irreversible. Neither can any mandate of public authority, which would seek to impose direct sterilization as necessary for the common good, be invoked, for such sterilization damages the dignity and inviolability of the human person. Likewise, neither can one invoke the principle of totality in this case, in virtue of which principle interference with organs is justified for the greater good of the person; sterility intended in itself is not oriented to the integral good of the person as rightly pursued, 'the proper order of goods being preserved,' inasmuch as it damages the ethical good of the person, which is the highest good, since it deliberately deprives foreseen and freely chosen sexual activity of an essential element" (Congregation for the Doctrine of the Faith, *Responses to Questions concerning Sterilization in Catholic Hospitals* [March 13, 1975], n. 1: *AAS* 68 [1976], 738–739).

must be rejected,[53] inasmuch as it contradicts the inviolability of the human person and of his physical integrity by precluding openness to life.[54]

Sterilization resulting from therapeutic acts

Sterilization resulting from a therapeutic act is a different case, which does not raise moral problems. It is legitimate on the basis of the principle of totality, whereby it is lawful to deprive a person of an organ or of its functioning when it is sick or is the cause of pathological processes that are not otherwise curable. There must also be a foreseeable and reasonable benefit for the patient, and he himself or his legal guardians must have given consent.

No to compulsory sterilization

21.   Compulsory sterilization is imposed by an authority on specific persons or groups of persons for eugenic reasons (as in the case of preventing hereditary illnesses), for the protection of society (as might be claimed in the case of sterilizing recidivous rapists), for the purported protection of frail or vulnerable persons, or for other reasons. Such sterilization, having no therapeutic character whatsoever, injures the person's dignity and physical integrity and his right to procreate in marriage. As such, it is morally illicit.[55]

Human and Christian understanding of sexuality

22.   Suitably trained health care workers, in accordance with the opportunities available to them, can help promote a human and Christian understanding of sexuality by informing and educating young people about natural methods in the wider context of a sound education about sexuality and love, and by making accessible to spouses the necessary knowledge for responsible behavior that is respectful of the unique dignity of human sexuality.[56]

---

53 Cf. Paul VI, Encyclical Letter *Humanae vitae*, n. 14: *AAS* 60 (1968), 490.

54 Cf. ibid., n. 17: *AAS* 60 (1968), 493–494.

55 Cf. ibid.

56 Cf. John Paul II, Apostolic Exhortation *Familiaris consortio*, n. 33: *AAS* 74 (1982), 120–123.

The establishment of appropriate centers for the natural regulation of fertility can be of great assistance in providing correct instruction in natural methods. Such centers "should be promoted as a valuable help to responsible parenthood, in which all individuals, and in the first place the child, are recognized and respected in their own right, and where every decision is guided by the ideal of the sincere gift of self."[57] For these reasons, the Church appeals to health care workers to be suitably trained in this specific field and to feel responsible for "actually help[ing] married people to live their love with respect for the structure and finalities of the conjugal act which expresses that love."[58]

Centers for the natural regulation of fertility

Medical responses to marital infertility

23.   The application to human beings of biotechnologies derived from animal fertilization has made possible various interventions on human procreation, raising serious questions about moral permissibility. "The various *techniques of artificial reproduction*, which would seem to be at the service of life and which are frequently used with this intention, actually open the door to new threats against life."[59]

As far as *treating infertility* is concerned, the new medical techniques must respect three fundamental goods: (1) the right to life and to physical integrity of every human being from conception until natural death; (2) the unity of marriage, which involves mutual respect for the right of spouses to become parents only through each other; (3) the specifically human values of sexuality, which require "that the procreation of a human person be brought

Criteria for treating infertility

---

57   John Paul II, Encyclical Letter *Evangelium vitae*, n. 88: *AAS* 87 (1995), 500–501.

58   John Paul II, Apostolic Exhortation *Familiaris consortio*, n. 35: *AAS* 74 (1982), 125.

59   John Paul II, Encyclical Letter *Evangelium vitae*, n. 14: *AAS* 87 (1995), 416.

about as the fruit of the conjugal act specific to the love between spouses."[60]

Conjugal act as the expression of a reciprocal gift

This personal act is the intimate union of love by the spouses, who by giving themselves to each other totally, give life. It is one indivisible act, both unitive and procreative, conjugal and parental, "the expression of the reciprocal gift which, according to Holy Scripture, effects the union 'in one flesh'":[61] it is the center from which new life can issue.

24.   Man cannot disregard the meanings and values that are intrinsic to human life from its very beginning. The dignity of the human person requires that it come into existence as the fruit of a conjugal act. Conjugal love, indeed, expresses its fruitfulness in the generation of life through the act that reflects and embodies the unitive and procreative dimensions of the spouses' love.

Assist but never replace the conjugal act

Every medical means and intervention, in the area of procreation, must function in such a way as to assist but never to replace the conjugal act. Indeed, "the doctor is at the service of persons and of human procreation. He does not have the authority to dispose of them or to decide their fate. A medical intervention respects the dignity of persons when it seeks to assist the conjugal act either to facilitate its performance or to enable it to achieve its objective once it has been normally performed. On the other hand, it sometimes happens that a medical procedure technologically replaces the conjugal act in order to obtain a procreation which is neither its result nor its fruit. In this case the medical act is not, as it should be, at the service of conjugal union but rather appropriates to itself the procreative function and thus contradicts the dignity

---

60 Congregation for the Doctrine of the Faith, Instruction *Dignitas personae*, n. 12: *AAS* 100 (2008), 865.

61 Pius XII, Discourse to the Italian Catholic Union of Midwives (October 29, 1951): *AAS* 43 (1951), 850.

and the inalienable rights of the spouses and of the child to be born."[62]

25.   Interventions that aim to remove obstacles to natural fertility,[63] or that are intended solely either to facilitate the natural act or to bring about the attainment of the proper end of the natural act as it is performed normally, are certainly licit. This may be the case with homologous artificial insemination, within marriage, with the husband's semen, when it is obtained through the normal conjugal act and the temporal continuity between the conjugal act and conception is respected.[64]

Homologous insemination within marriage

26.   Illicit procedures include homologous in vitro fertilization and embryo transfer (IVF-ET), in which conception occurs not within the mother but outside of her body, in vitro, through the work of technicians who determine the conditions thereof and make the decision to bring it about.[65]

No to homologous IVF-ET

In itself the extracorporeal technique "dissociates from the conjugal act"—which is "an act that is inseparably corporal and spiritual"—"the actions which are directed to

---

62   Congregation for the Doctrine of the Faith, Instruction *Donum vitae*, II, B, 7: *AAS* 80 (1988), 96.

63   Cf. Congregation for the Doctrine of the Faith, Instruction *Dignitas personae*, n. 13: *AAS* 100 (2008), 866. These cases include, for example, hormonal treatment for infertility of gonadal origin, surgical treatment of endometriosis, clearing of a blockage in the fallopian tubes, or microsurgery to restore the patency of a tube.

64   Cf. ibid., n. 12: *AAS* 100 (2008), 866.

65   "Homologous IVF and ET is brought about outside the bodies of the couple through actions of third parties whose competence and technical activity determine the success of the procedure. Such fertilization entrusts the life and identity of the embryo to the power of doctors and biologists and establishes the domination of technology over the origin and destiny of the human person" (Congregation for the Doctrine of the Faith, Instruction *Donum vitae*, II, B, 5: *AAS* 80 [1988], 93).

human fertilization."[66] Indeed, "fertilization is neither in fact achieved nor positively willed as the expression and fruit of a specific act of the conjugal union,"[67] but rather as the "result" of a technological intervention. This does not correspond to the logic of "donation" which human generation implies, but rather to the logic of "production" and "dominion" that pertains to objects and effects. Here the child is not born as a "gift" of love, but as a laboratory "product."[68]

In these cases, in fact, man "no longer considers life as a splendid gift of God, something 'sacred' entrusted to his responsibility and thus also to his loving care and 'veneration.' Life itself becomes a mere 'thing,' which man claims as his exclusive property, completely subject to his control and manipulation."[69]

Difference between desire for a child and right to a child

27.   The spouses' desire for a child, however sincere and intense it may be, does not legitimize recourse to techniques

---

66 Congregation for the Doctrine of the Faith, Instruction *Donum vitae*, II, B, 4, 5: *AAS* 80 (1988), 91, 92–94. "Just as in general with in vitro fertilization, of which it is a variety, ICSI [intracytoplasmic sperm injection] is intrinsically illicit: it causes a complete separation between procreation and the conjugal act" (Congregation for the Doctrine of the Faith, Instruction *Dignitas personae*, n. 17: *AAS* 100 [2008], 870).

67 Congregation for the Doctrine of the Faith, Instruction *Dignitas personae*, n. 17: *AAS* 100 (2008), 870.

68 Cf. Congregation for the Doctrine of the Faith, Instruction *Donum vitae*, II: *AAS* 80 (1988), 85–86, 91–92, 96–97. "In reality, the origin of a human person is the result of an act of giving. The one conceived must be the fruit of his parents' love. He cannot be desired or conceived as the product of an intervention of medical or biological techniques; that would be equivalent to reducing him to an object of scientific technology. No one may subject the coming of a child into the world to conditions of technical efficiency which are to be evaluated according to standards of control and dominion" (*Donum vitae*, II, B, 4c: *AAS* 80 [1988], 92).

69 John Paul II, Encyclical Letter *Evangelium vitae*, n. 22: *AAS* 87 (1995), 425.

that are contrary to the truth of human generation and to the dignity of the new human being.[70]

The desire for a child does not give rise to any right to a child. A child is a person, with the dignity of a "subject." As such he cannot be willed as an "object" of a right. Rather, the child is the subject of rights: it is the child's right to be conceived with full respect for the fact that he is a person.[71]

28.   Besides these reasons that are intrinsically contrary to the dignity of the human person and of his conception, circumstances and consequences related to the technical means of execution contribute to making techniques of extracorporeal artificial fertilization morally unacceptable.

Aggravating circumstances associated with IVF

These techniques in fact involve *the loss of many embryos*. Some of these losses result from the techniques themselves, whereby the loss of around 80 percent of the

---

70 Cf. Congregation for the Doctrine of the Faith, Instruction *Donum vitae*, II, B, 5: *AAS* 80 (1988), 93.

71 Cf. Ibid., II, B, 8: *AAS* 80 (1988), 97. "A child is not something *owed* to one, but is a *gift*. The 'supreme gift of marriage' is a human person. A child may not be considered a piece of property, an idea to which an alleged 'right to a child' would lead. In this area, only the child possesses genuine rights: the right 'to be the fruit of the specific act of the conjugal love of his parents,' and 'the right to be respected as a person from the moment of his conception'" (*CCC*, n. 2378). "Certainly, homologous IVF and ET fertilization is not marked by all that ethical negativity found in extra-conjugal procreation; the family and marriage continue to constitute the setting for the birth and upbringing of the children. Nevertheless, in conformity with the traditional doctrine relating to the goods of marriage and the dignity of the person, the Church remains opposed from the moral point of view to homologous 'in vitro' fertilization. Such fertilization is in itself illicit and in opposition to the dignity of procreation and of the conjugal union, even when everything is done to avoid the death of the human embryo. Although the manner in which human conception is achieved with IVF and ET cannot be approved, every child which comes into the world must in any case be accepted as a living gift of the divine Goodness and must be brought up with love" (Congregation for the Doctrine of the Faith, Instruction *Donum vitae*, II, B, 5: *AAS* 80 [1988], 94).

embryos that are actually transferred is accepted in order to obtain the birth of one baby. Other embryos are eliminated directly because they have genetic defects.[72] Finally, in the case of a multiple pregnancy, one or more embryos or fetuses may be destroyed directly to reduce risks to the embryos or fetuses that are spared.[73] Every direct destruction of a human being between conception and birth has the character of an actual abortion in the moral sense.

In reference to the above-mentioned circumstances and consequences related to methods of extracorporeal artificial fertilization, we are therefore dealing with factors that aggravate a technical procedure which is already morally illicit in itself.

No to heterologous artificial fertilization techniques

29.   *Heterologous artificial fertilization techniques* are vitiated by the unethical character of engendering children apart from marriage. Recourse to the gametes of third persons (i.e., not from the husband or wife) is contrary to the unity of marriage and the fidelity of the spouses, and violates the right of the child to be conceived and brought into the world by the two spouses. In this case, procreation is welcomed "only because it expresses a desire, or indeed the intention, to have a child 'at all costs,' and not because it signifies the complete acceptance of the other and therefore an openness to the richness of life which the child represents."[74]

In fact, these techniques ignore the common, united vocation of the spouses to fatherhood and motherhood—"to become a father and a mother only through each other"—and bring about "a rupture between genetic parenthood, gestational parenthood, and responsibility for

72 Congregation for the Doctrine of the Faith, Instruction *Dignitas personae*, nn. 15, 22: *AAS* 100 (2008), 867, 873.

73 Ibid., n. 21: *AAS* 100 (2008), 872.

74 John Paul II, Encyclical Letter *Evangelium vitae*, n. 23: *AAS* 87 (1995), 427.

upbringing,"[75] which has repercussions not only in the family but also in society.

A further reason for condemning such techniques is the commodification and eugenic selection of gametes.

30. For the same reasons, aggravated by the absence of a marital bond, artificial fertilization for unmarried persons and for cohabiting couples is morally unacceptable.[76] "Thus the original import of human sexuality is distorted and falsified, and the two meanings, unitive and procreative, inherent in the very nature of the conjugal act, are artificially separated: in this way the marriage union is betrayed and its fruitfulness is subjected to the caprice of the couple."[77]

No to artificial fertilization for unmarried persons or cohabiting couples

For the same reasons, postmortem insemination, that is, with semen of the deceased husband that was obtained and stored during his lifetime, is contrary to the truth of procreation and to the dignity of the child to be born.

No to postmortem insemination

31. *Surrogate motherhood* is equally contrary to the dignity of the woman, to the unity of marriage, and to the dignity of the procreation of a human person.

No to surrogate motherhood

To impregnate a woman by fertilizing her own ovum with donor sperm or by implanting into a woman's uterus an embryo that is genetically foreign to her, and to make her promise to deliver the newborn child to a client, is to fragment motherhood, reducing gestation to a process of incubation that shows no respect for the child's dignity and "right to be conceived, carried in the womb, brought into the world and brought up within marriage."[78]

75 Congregation for the Doctrine of the Faith, Instruction *Donum vitae*, II, A, 1 and 2: *AAS* 80 (1988), 87–89.

76 Cf. ibid., II, A, 2: *AAS* 80 (1988), 88.

77 John Paul II, Encyclical Letter *Evangelium vitae*, n. 23: *AAS* 87 (1995), 427.

78 Congregation for the Doctrine of the Faith, Instruction *Donum vitae*, II, A, 1: *AAS* 80 (1988), 87.

*Accepting
life as a gift
from God*

32.   Although it is not possible to approve the method by which fertilization is brought about, "every child which comes into the world must in any case be accepted as a living gift of the divine Goodness and must be brought up with love."[79]

Prenatal and preimplantation diagnosis

*Ethical
problems
with prenatal
diagnosis*

33.   Our increasingly extensive knowledge about intra-uterine life and the development of tools to access it enable earlier possibilities of diagnosis for prenatal life, allowing ever more timely and effective therapeutic interventions. Prenatal diagnosis, however, can present ethical problems connected with diagnostic risk and with the purposes for which it is requested.

*Risk
assessment*

34.   Diagnostic risk concerns the life and physical integrity of the child who has been conceived, and those of the mother only to some degree, depending on the various diagnostic techniques and the percentages of risk associated with each one.

It is therefore necessary to evaluate carefully the possible negative consequences which the use of a particular exploratory technique may have and to "avoid recourse to diagnostic procedures which do not offer sufficient guarantees of their honest purpose and substantial harmlessness."[80] And if a degree of risk must be undertaken, there must be reasonable indications for recourse to diagnosis, which are to be verified in the course of diagnostic consultation.[81]

---

79   Ibid., II, B, 5: *AAS* 80 (1988), 92–93.

80   John Paul II, Discourse to participants in the Pro-Life Movement Congress (December 3, 1982), n. 4: *Insegnamenti* V/3 (1982), 1512.

81   Cf. John Paul II, Encyclical Letter *Evangelium vitae*, n. 63: *AAS* 87 (1995), 473; John Paul II, Discourse to participants in the Pro-Life Movement Congress, n. 4: *Insegnamenti* V/3 (1982), 1512.

Consequently, "such diagnosis is permissible, with the consent of the parents after they have been adequately informed, if the methods employed safeguard the life and integrity of the embryo and the mother, without subjecting them to disproportionate risks."[82]

Permissible prenatal diagnosis: proportionate risks

35.   The *purposes* for which prenatal diagnosis may be requested and performed must always be *for the benefit* of the child and of the mother, whether they are directed to the enabling of therapeutic interventions, to providing certainty and peace of mind to pregnant women who are anxious about the possibility of fetal malformations and are tempted to resort to abortion, or in the case of an unfavorable outcome, to preparing them to welcome the life of a child with a handicap.

Prenatal diagnosis that is opposed to the moral law

Prenatal diagnosis "is gravely opposed to the moral law when it is done with the thought of possibly inducing an abortion depending upon the results: a diagnosis which shows the existence of a malformation or a hereditary illness must not be the equivalent of a death sentence."[83]

Connection between prenatal diagnosis and abortion

Also illicit is any rule or policy proposed in legislation or by scientific societies that promotes a direct connection between prenatal diagnosis and abortion. Any specialist who, in deciding on and conducting the diagnosis and communicating the results, deliberately helps to establish or promote a link between prenatal diagnosis and abortion would be guilty of immoral cooperation.[84]

---

82   Congregation for the Doctrine of the Faith, Instruction *Donum vitae*, I, 2: *AAS* 80 (1988), 79.

83   Ibid.: *AAS* 80 (1988), 79–80. "Prenatal diagnosis, which presents no moral objections if carried out in order to identify the medical treatment which may be needed by the child in the womb, all too often becomes an opportunity for proposing and procuring an abortion. This is eugenic abortion, ... on the basis of a mentality ... which accepts life only under certain conditions and rejects it when it is affected by any limitation, handicap or illness" (John Paul II, Encyclical Letter *Evangelium vitae*, n. 14: *AAS* 87 [1995], 416).

84   Congregation for the Doctrine of the Faith, Instruction *Donum vitae*, I, 2: *AAS* 80 (1988), 79–80.

*Preimplant-
ation genetic
diagnosis
and eugenic
mentality*

36.   *Preimplantation genetic diagnosis* is a particular form of prenatal diagnosis. It is connected to extracorporeal artificial fertilization techniques and involves the genetic diagnosis of embryos that are engendered in vitro before they are transferred to the uterus, in order to selectively use embryos without genetic defects or with desired characteristics.[85] Preimplantation genetic diagnosis is in fact an expression of a eugenic mentality that legitimizes selective abortion to prevent the birth of babies afflicted with various illnesses.

"Such an attitude is shameful and utterly reprehensible, since it presumes to measure the value of a human life only within the parameters of 'normality' and physical well-being, thus opening the way to legitimizing infanticide and euthanasia as well."[86] This procedure, therefore, "is directed toward the *qualitative selection and consequent destruction of embryos*, which constitutes an act of abortion."[87]

Freezing embryos and oocytes

*No to cryo-
preservation
of embryos*

37.   In vitro fertilization techniques often require repeated attempts before obtaining a result. Many oocytes are therefore obtained from the woman in a single intervention in order to obtain multiple embryos. The embryos that are not immediately transferred are frozen for potential use in a later attempt. "Cryopreservation is *incompatible with the respect owed to human embryos*: it presupposes their

---

85   Preimplantation diagnosis is applied today in a growing number of situations, besides the simple elimination of embryos with genetic or chromosomal anomalies. It is the case, for example, with the elimination of aneuploid embryos so as to improve the success rate of IVF-ET, especially in postmenopausal women. It is also the case with choosing an embryo because of its sex or selecting an embryo as a future donor of umbilical stem cells or of bone marrow based on compatibility with a patient who is already born.

86   Congregation for the Doctrine of the Faith, Instruction *Dignitas personae*, n. 22: *AAS* 100 (2008), 873–874.

87   Ibid.: *AAS* 100 (2008), 873.

production in vitro; it exposes them to the serious risk of death or physical harm, since a high percentage do not survive the process of freezing and thawing; it deprives them at least temporarily of maternal reception and gestation; it places them in a situation in which they are susceptible to further offense and manipulation."[88]

The enormous number of frozen embryos that exist, many of which are doomed to become "orphans," raises the question of what to do with them after their storage time has expired. They cannot be used for research or designated for therapeutic purposes, because that would involve their destruction. The proposal to move forward with a form of prenatal adoption, "praiseworthy with regard to the intention of respecting and defending human life, presents however various problems,"[89] medical, psychological, and legal, not unlike those caused by heterologous techniques and by surrogate motherhood. "All things considered, it needs to be recognized that the thousands of abandoned embryos represent *a situation of injustice which in fact cannot be resolved*,"[90] and therefore the practice of cryopreservation must be stopped as soon as possible.

Injustice that cannot be resolved

38.   To avoid the serious ethical problems caused by the cryopreservation of embryos, techniques have been developed for freezing oocytes. The cryopreservation of human egg cells for the purpose of in vitro fertilization is unacceptable, even when the reasoning behind cryopreservation is to protect the oocytes from an antitumor therapy that is potentially harmful to them.

No to cryopreservation of oocytes

It would be a different matter to preserve ovarian tissue for use in an orthotopic autograft transplant, so as to restore fertility after treatments that are potentially harmful to the oocytes. This practice, in principle, appears to pose no moral problems.

Preservation of ovarian tissue

---

88   Ibid., n. 18: *AAS* 100 (2008), 870.
89   Ibid., n. 19: *AAS* 100 (2008), 871.
90   Ibid.

New attempts at human generation and procreation

Other procedures contrary to the dignity of the embryo

39.   Artificial fertilization techniques today may pave the way for attempts at or plans for fertilization using human and animal gametes; for the gestation of human embryos in animal or artificial uteruses; and for the asexual reproduction of human beings by means of twin fission, cloning, parthenogenesis, or similar techniques. These procedures are contrary to the human dignity of the embryo and of procreation, and therefore should be considered morally reprehensible.[91]

In particular, *cloning for reproductive purposes* must be considered "intrinsically illicit in that, by taking the ethical negativity of techniques of artificial fertilization to their extreme, it seeks to *give rise to a new human being without a connection to the act of reciprocal self-giving between the spouses and*, more radically, *without any link to sexuality*."[92]

"From the ethical point of view, so-called *therapeutic cloning* is even more serious. To create embryos with the intention of destroying them, even with the intention of helping the sick, is completely incompatible with human dignity, because it makes the existence of a human being at the embryonic stage nothing more than a means to be used and destroyed. It is *gravely immoral to sacrifice a human life for therapeutic ends*."[93]

In the case of so-called *hybrid cloning*, in which animal oocytes are used to reprogram human somatic cells, there is a further "offense against the dignity of human beings on account of *the admixture of human and animal genetic elements capable of disrupting the specific identity of man*."[94]

---

91   Cf. Congregation for the Doctrine of the Faith, Instruction *Donum vitae*, II, B, 7: *AAS* 80 (1988), 95–96.

92   Congregation for the Doctrine of the Faith, Instruction *Dignitas personae*, n. 28: *AAS* 100 (2008), 879.

93   Ibid., n. 30: *AAS* 100 (2008), 879.

94   Ibid., n. 33: *AAS* 100 (2008), 882.

LIVING

40. "From the time that the ovum is fertilized, a life is begun which is neither that of the father nor of the mother; it is rather the life of a new human being with his own growth. It would never be made human if it were not human already. ... The adventure of a human life is begun right from fertilization, and each of its capacities requires time—a rather lengthy time—to find its place and to be in a position to act."[95]

Beginning of a new human individual

The findings of human biology confirm that "in the zygote resulting from fertilization the biological identity of a new human individual is already constituted."[96] This is the individuality belonging to a being that is autonomous, intrinsically determined, and self-realizing with gradual continuity.

Personal nature of the zygote

It is therefore erroneous and misleading to speak about a "pre-embryo," if by that term is meant a state or condition of pre-human life of the human being who has been conceived. "The reality of the human being for the entire span of life, both before and after birth, does not allow us to posit either a change in nature or a gradation in moral value, since it possesses *full anthropological and ethical status*. The human embryo has, therefore, from the very beginning, the dignity proper to a person."[97] His soul, irreducible to mere matter, can have its origin in God alone, inasmuch as it is created directly by Him and is the principle of the unity of the human being,[98] and the seed of

---

95 Congregation for the Doctrine of the Faith, *Declaration on Procured Abortion* (November 18, 1974), nn. 12–13: *AAS* 66 (1974), 738.

96 Congregation for the Doctrine of the Faith, Instruction *Donum vitae*, I, 1: *AAS* 80 (1988), 78.

97 Congregation for the Doctrine of the Faith, Instruction *Dignitas personae*, n. 5: *AAS* 100 (2008), 862.

98 Cf. Vatican Council II, Pastoral Constitution *Gaudium et spes*, n. 14. "The spiritual and immortal soul is the principle of unity of the human being, whereby it exists as a whole—*corpore et anima unus*—as a person" (John Paul II, Encyclical Letter *Veritatis splendor*, n. 48: *AAS* 85 [1993], 1172).

eternity that he bears within himself.[99] "How can anyone think that even a single moment of this marvelous process of the unfolding of life could be separated from the wise and loving work of the Creator, and left prey to human caprice?"[100]

41.   Prenatal life is fully human life at every stage of its development. It is owed therefore the same respect, the same protection, and the same care that are due to a human person.

Careful watch over nascent life

All social workers and health care workers, in particular those who carry out their service in obstetrics departments, "must keep a careful watch over the wonderful and mysterious process of generation taking place in the maternal womb, to ensure its normal development and successful outcome with the birth of the new child."[101]

Transition from gestation to physiological independence

42.   The *birth* of a baby marks an important and significant moment in the development that began with conception, inasmuch as the baby from that moment on is capable of living in physiological independence from the mother and of entering into a new relation with the external world.

It can happen, in the case of a premature birth, that this independence has not been fully attained. In that event, however, health care workers have the obligation to assist the newborn and to implement appropriate care and treatments aimed at achieving viability or else, if that

---

99   Cf. *CCC*, n. 33. "Although the presence of the spiritual soul cannot be observed experimentally, the conclusions of science regarding the human embryo give 'a valuable indication for discerning by the use of reason a personal presence at the moment of the first appearance of a human life: how could a human individual not be a human person?'" (Congregation for the Doctrine of the Faith, Instruction *Dignitas personae*, n. 5: *AAS* 100 [2008], 862).

100   John Paul II, Encyclical Letter *Evangelium vitae*, n. 44: *AAS* 87 (1995), 450.

101   John Paul II, Address to the participants in a congress for obstetricians (January 26, 1980), n. 1: *AAS* 72 (1980), 84.

is not possible, to accompany him in the final phase of his life.

43.   When there is fear for the life of the newborn, health care workers, as sharers in the evangelizing mission entrusted to the Church (cf. Mt 28:19; Mk 16:15–16), can administer baptism according to the prescribed conditions.[102]

Baptism in danger of death

44.   Respect, protection and care are owed to every human being, "because each one carries in an indelible way his own dignity and value."[103] Man, in fact, is the only creature on earth that God "willed for his own sake"; his whole being bears the image of the Creator. Consequently, human life is sacred, "because from its beginning it involves 'the creative action of God' and it remains forever in a special relationship with the Creator, who is its sole end."[104] Therefore every human being, from the very beginning, has the dignity and value proper to a person.[105]

The unique dignity of human beings

45.   Human life is at the same time, and irreducibly, corporeal and spiritual. "By virtue of its substantial union with a spiritual soul, the human body cannot be considered as a mere complex of tissues, organs and functions, nor can it be evaluated in the same way as the body of animals; rather, it is a constitutive part of the person who manifests and expresses himself through it."[106]

Bodily and spiritual life

46.   The body, the manifestation of the person, is not ethically indifferent, but rather has moral relevance: it is both indicative and imperative with respect to human

The body: manifestation of the person

---

102   Cf. *Code of Canon Law* (*CIC*), can. 861 §2.
103   Congregation for the Doctrine of the Faith, Instruction *Dignitas personae*, n. 6: *AAS* 100 (2008), 862.
104   Congregation for the Doctrine of the Faith, Instruction *Donum vitae*, n. 5: *AAS* 80 (1988), 76–77.
105   Cf. Congregation for the Doctrine of the Faith, Instruction *Dignitas personae*, n. 5: *AAS* 100 (2008), 861-862.
106   Congregation for the Doctrine of the Faith, Instruction *Donum vitae*, n. 3: *AAS* 80 (1988), 74.

action.[107] The human body is "a properly personal reality, a sign and place of relations with others, with God, and with the world."[108]

The body has its own laws and values, which man must gradually discover, employ, and set in order. It is not possible to prescind from the body and set up subjective feelings and desires as the exclusive criterion and source of morality.

Human life inviolable and "indisposable"

Body belonging to God

47.   "The inviolability of the person, which is a reflection of the absolute inviolability of God, finds its primary and fundamental expression in the *inviolability of human life*."[109] "The question, 'What have you done?' (Gen 4:10), which God addresses to Cain after Cain has killed his brother Abel, interprets the experience of every person: in the depths of his conscience, man is always reminded of the inviolability of life—his own life and that of others—as something which does not belong to him, because it is the property and gift of God the Creator and Father."[110]

---

107 "For it is only in keeping with his true nature that the human person can achieve self-realization as a 'unified totality': and this nature is at the same time corporal and spiritual. By virtue of its substantial union with a spiritual soul, the human body cannot be considered as a mere complex of tissues, organs and functions, nor can it be evaluated in the same way as the body of animals; rather it is a constitutive part of the person who manifests and expresses himself through it. The natural moral law expresses and lays down the purposes, rights and duties which are based upon the bodily and spiritual nature of the human person. Therefore this law cannot be thought of as simply a set of norms on the biological level; rather it must be defined as the rational order whereby man is called by the Creator to direct and regulate his life and actions and in particular to make use of his own body" (Congregation for the Doctrine of the Faith, Instruction *Donum vitae*, n. 3: *AAS* 80 [1988], 74). Cf. Paul VI, Encyclical Letter *Humanae vitae*, n. 10: *AAS* 60 (1968), 487.

108 Cf. John Paul II, Encyclical Letter *Evangelium vitae*, n. 23: *AAS* 87 (1995), 426.

109 John Paul II, Apostolic Exhortation *Christifideles laici*, n. 38: *AAS* 81 (1989), 462–463.

110 John Paul II, Encyclical Letter *Evangelium vitae*, n. 40: *AAS* 87 (1995), 445.

The body shares inseparably with the soul in the dignity and human value belonging to the person: it is a *body-subject* and not a body-object, and as such it is inviolable and "indisposable."[111] One cannot dispose of the body at will like a piece of property, just as one cannot manipulate it as a thing or an instrument over which one is the master and arbiter.

Offense against the dignity of the person

Every improper intervention on the body is an offense against the dignity of the person and therefore against God, who is the one, absolute Lord of it: "The human being is not master of his own life: he receives it in order to use it; he is not the proprietor but the administrator, because God alone is Lord of life."[112]

48.   The fact that life belongs to God, and not to man, confers on it the sacred character that elicits an attitude of profound respect: "Human life is sacred because from its beginning it involves 'the creative action of God' and it remains forever in a special relationship with the Creator, who is its sole end. God alone is the Lord of life from its beginning until its end: no one can, in any circumstance, claim for himself the right to destroy directly an innocent human being."[113]

Sacred character of life

Medical practice and health care facilities are above all supposed to serve and protect this sacredness of human life: a profession in defense of the noninstrumental value of life, which is a good in itself.[114] "Man's life comes from God; it is his gift, his image and imprint, a sharing in

111   "The human body shares in the dignity of 'the image of God': it is a human body precisely because it is animated by a spiritual soul, and it is the whole human person that is intended to become, in the body of Christ, a temple of the Spirit" (*CCC*, n. 364).
112   John Paul II, Address to the participants in a congress of the "Movement for Life" (October 12, 1985), n. 2: *AAS* 78 (1986), 265.
113   Congregation for the Doctrine of the Faith, Instruction *Donum vitae*, n. 5: *AAS* 80 (1988), 76–77.
114   "Scientists and doctors must not think that they are lords of life, but rather its expert and generous servants" (John Paul II, Address to the Pontifical Academy of Sciences [October 21, 1985], n. 3: *AAS* 78 [1986], 277).

his breath of life. God therefore is the sole Lord of this life: man cannot do with it as he wills."[115]

49.   This has to be declared with particular force and accepted deliberately and vigilantly in a time of invasive developments in biomedical technologies, in which the danger of the abusive manipulation of human life is increasing. At issue here are not the techniques in themselves but their presumed ethical neutrality. Not everything that is technically possible can be considered morally admissible.

Technological possibilities and ethical permissibility

Technological possibilities must be measured by the standard of ethical permissibility, which determines their human compatibility or, in other words, whether they effectively safeguard and respect the dignity of the human person.[116]

Science: an ally to wisdom

50.   Science and technology make new advances every day, but "they cannot of themselves show the meaning of existence and of human progress. Being ordered to man, who initiates and develops them, they draw from the person and his moral values the indication of their purpose and the awareness of their limits."[117] This is why science must be an ally to wisdom.[118]

---

115   John Paul II, Encyclical Letter *Evangelium vitae*, n. 39: *AAS* 87 (1995), 444.

116   John Paul II, Address to the participants in a congress of the "Movement for Life" (October 12, 1985), n. 5: *AAS* 78 (1986), 267; John Paul II, Address to the participants in a congress of the Pontifical Academy of Sciences (October 23, 1982), n. 2: *AAS* 75 (1983), 36; John Paul II, Address to the participants in the Colloquium of the International Foundation *Nova spes* (November 9, 1987), n. 2: *AAS* 80 (1988), 627.

117   Congregation for the Doctrine of the Faith, Instruction *Donum vitae*, n. 2: *AAS* 80 (1988), 73.

118   Cf. Congregation for the Doctrine of the Faith, Instruction *Dignitas personae*, n. 10: *AAS* 100 (2008), 864.

Abortion and the destruction of nascent life

51.   The inviolability of the human person from the moment of conception forbids abortion, which is the destruction of prenatal life and a direct violation of the human being's fundamental right to life: "The fruit of human procreation, from the first moment of its existence, must be guaranteed that unconditional respect which is morally due to the human being in his or her totality and unity as body and spirit: '*The human being is to be respected and treated as a person from the moment of conception*; and therefore from that same moment his rights as a person must be recognized, among which in the first place is the inviolable right of every innocent human being to life.'"[119]

No to abortion

The deliberate destruction of nascent life is, therefore, an "unspeakable crime":[120] "*Direct abortion, that is, abortion willed as an end or as a means, always constitutes a grave moral disorder*, since it is the deliberate killing of an innocent human being. ... No circumstance, no purpose, no law whatsoever can ever make licit an act which is intrinsically illicit, since it is contrary to the Law of God which is written in every human heart, knowable by reason itself, and proclaimed by the Church."[121]

The elimination of the life of an unwanted unborn child has become a rather widespread phenomenon, financed by public funding and facilitated by permissive laws that either decriminalize or legalize procured abortion.[122] All this inevitably leads many people to stop taking

No to cultural acceptance of abortion

119   John Paul II, Encyclical Letter *Evangelium vitae*, n. 60: *AAS* 87 (1995), 469.

120   Vatican Council II, Pastoral Constitution *Gaudium et spes*, n. 51. Cf. Paul VI, Address to participants in the Twenty-Third National Convention of the Union of Italian Catholic Lawyers (December 9, 1972): *AAS* 64 (1972), 776–779.

121   John Paul II, Encyclical Letter *Evangelium vitae*, n. 62: *AAS* 87 (1995), 472.

122   "Among the vulnerable for whom the Church wishes to care with particular love and concern are unborn children, the most defenseless and innocent among us. Nowadays efforts are made

any responsibility for nascent life and to trivialize abortion and ignore its moral gravity.[123]

52.   The Church raises her voice in defense of life, in particular life that is defenseless and ignored, such as embryonic and fetal life.[124] The Church, therefore, calls

Professional integrity

health care workers to *professional integrity*, which tolerates no action that destroys life, despite "the risk of incomprehension, misunderstandings, and even weighty

to deny them their human dignity and to do with them whatever one pleases, taking their lives and passing laws preventing anyone from standing in the way of this. Frequently, as a way of ridiculing the Church's effort to defend their lives, attempts are made to present her position as ideological, obscurantist and conservative. Yet this defense of unborn life is closely linked to the defense of each and every other human right. It [presupposes] the conviction that a human being is always sacred and inviolable, in any situation and at every stage of development. Human beings are ends in themselves and never a means of resolving other problems. Once this conviction disappears, so do solid and lasting foundations for the defense of human rights, which would always be subject to the passing whims of the powers that be" (Francis, Apostolic Exhortation *Evangelii gaudium*, n. 213). Cf. John Paul II, Address to participants in a convention of the "Movement for Life" (October 12, 1985), n. 3: *AAS* 78 (1986), 266.

123   "Unfortunately, this disturbing state of affairs, far from decreasing, is expanding. ... [A] new cultural climate is developing and taking hold, which gives crimes against life *a new and—if possible— even more sinister character*, giving rise to further grave concern: broad sectors of public opinion justify certain crimes against life in the name of the rights of individual freedom, and on this basis they claim not only exemption from punishment but even authorization by the State, so that these things can be done with total freedom and indeed with the free assistance of health care systems" (John Paul II, Encyclical Letter *Evangelium vitae*, n. 4: *AAS* 87 [1995], 404). Cf. *CCC*, n. 2271.

124   "Reason alone is sufficient to recognize the inviolable value of each single human life, but if we also look at the issue from the standpoint of faith, 'every violation of the personal dignity of the human being cries out in vengeance to God and is an offense against the creator of the individual'" (Francis, Apostolic Exhortation *Evangelii gaudium*, n. 213).

acts of discrimination"[125] that this coherence may involve. *Medical and health care integrity* declares illegitimate any surgical or pharmaceutical intervention aimed at interrupting pregnancy at any stage.

53.   It is understandable that, in certain cases, refraining from abortion might be seen to conflict with goods that are deemed important and worth safeguarding, as in the case of serious danger to the health of the mother, gravely challenging socioeconomic situations, or a pregnancy that originated in sexual violence.[126]

Assessing extreme situations

We cannot ignore or minimize these difficulties and the reasons that give rise to them. It is necessary, however, to affirm that none of them can confer the right to dispose of the life of another person, even in its initial phase: there are no exceptions to the moral norm that prohibits the direct destruction of an innocent human being.[127]

54.   Any form of direct abortion is ethically illegitimate inasmuch as it is an intrinsically reprehensible act. When abortion is neither intended nor willed but follows as a foreseen consequence of a therapeutic act that is inescapably necessary for the health of the mother, this

Abortion as a consequence of a therapeutic act

125 John Paul II, Address to the Association of Italian Catholic Physicians (December 28, 1978): *Insegnamenti* I (1978), 439; cf. Congregation for the Doctrine of the Faith, *Declaration on Procured Abortion*, n. 24: *AAS* 66 (1974), 744.

126 "Precisely because this involves the internal consistency of our message about the value of the human person, the Church cannot be expected to change her position on this question. I want to be completely honest in this regard. This is not something subject to alleged reforms or 'modernizations.' It is not 'progressive' to try to resolve problems by eliminating a human life. On the other hand, it is also true that we have done little to adequately accompany women in very difficult situations, where abortion appears as a quick solution to their profound anguish, especially when the life developing within them is the result of rape or a situation of extreme poverty" (Francis, Apostolic Exhortation *Evangelii gaudium*, n. 214).

127 Cf. John Paul II, Encyclical Letter *Evangelium vitae*, n. 57: *AAS* 87 (1995), 466; Congregation for the Doctrine of the Faith, *Declaration on Procured Abortion*, n. 14: *AAS* 66 (1974), 740.

may be morally legitimate. In such a case, the abortion is the indirect consequence of an act that in itself is not a direct abortion.[128]

Embryo reduction

No to embryo reduction

55.　　Recent artificial reproduction techniques, especially the transfer of several embryos into the mother's womb, give rise to significant increases in multiple pregnancies, opening the way for possible interventions to reduce the number of embryos or fetuses present in the mother's womb by directly destroying them.

"From the ethical point of view, *embryo reduction is an intentional selective abortion.* It is in fact the deliberate and direct elimination of one or more innocent human beings in the initial phase of their existence and as such it always constitutes a grave moral disorder."[129]

Interception and contragestation

No to interception

56.　　There are several so-called *interceptive methods*[130] which, after conception has occurred, can prevent implantation of the embryo in the mother's womb. They do not in fact cause an abortion every time, because fertilization does not always occur after sexual relations.

Even when fertilization and the resulting abortion did not take place, the intention alone to prescribe and to employ these means for the purpose of preventing any

---

128　Cf. Pius XII, Address to "Face of the Family" and the Associations of Large Families (November 27, 1951): *AAS* 43 (1951), 859.

129　Congregation for the Doctrine of the Faith, Instruction *Dignitas personae*, n. 21: *AAS* 100 (2008), 872–873. Cf. Vatican Council II, Pastoral Constitution *Gaudium et spes*, n. 51; John Paul II, Encyclical Letter *Evangelium vitae*, n. 62: *AAS* 87 (1995), 472.

130　The most common interceptive methods are the intrauterine device (IUD) and the so-called morning-after pill.

embryo that may have been conceived from implanting in the uterus makes such acts abortive in a moral sense.[131]

Contragestive methods,[132] on the other hand, which cause the elimination of an already implanted embryo, always amount to direct abortion. "Therefore, the use of means of interception and contragestation fall within the *sin of abortion* and are gravely immoral."[133]

No to contra-gestation

Ectopic pregnancies

57.   The not infrequent pathologic condition of *ectopic pregnancy*, in which the implantation of the embryo occurs in a site other than the uterine cavity, not only poses clinical challenges but also has ethical implications. The woman may face a serious risk to her life or suffer consequences for her future fertility, while the embryo as a rule cannot survive. Here the applicable norm prohibits interventions to directly destroy the embryo, while it justifies interventions aimed exclusively at preserving the life and health of the woman that result in the embryo's demise.

No to directly destructive interventions for ectopic pregnancies

Anencephalic fetuses

58.   Another concern involves *anencephalic fetuses*, in which the brainstem is usually present but the cerebral hemispheres fail to develop. Many anencephalic fetuses die before delivery, and the rate of survival after birth is very low. It is not lawful to procure an abortion because the condition of anencephaly has been ascertained. The pregnant woman must be adequately supported and accompanied in this difficult experience.

No to abortion for anencephalic fetuses

At birth, these infants must receive only ordinary care, including palliative care, while avoiding any form of

---

131   Since generally the abortifacient effect cannot be ascertained, excommunication is not incurred. Cf. *CIC*, can. 1398.

132   The main methods of contragestation are the RU-486 pill, or mifepristone, prostaglandins, and methotrexate.

133   Congregation for the Doctrine of the Faith, Instruction *Dignitas personae*, n. 23: *AAS* 100 (2008), 875.

excessively burdensome or truly futile intervention. The eventual removal of organs or tissues is permissible only after death has been certified. Resuscitation of the infants for the sole purpose of maintaining their organs for procurement is not ethically justifiable, inasmuch as it is a form of exploitation that offends against their dignity as persons.[134]

Conscientious objection

Right and duty of conscientious objection

59.   When the law permits abortion, health care workers "must refuse politely but firmly."[135] A human being can never obey an intrinsically immoral law, as is the case with a law that admitted, as a matter of principle, that abortion is licit. The force of the inviolability of human life and of God's law, which defends it, precedes any positive human law.[136] When human law contradicts it, conscience affirms its primary right and the primacy of God's law: "We must obey God rather than men" (Acts 5:29).

Supremacy of God's law

Uprightness and fortitude in the truth

"Following one's conscience in obedience to the law of God is not always the easy way. One must not fail to recognize the weight of the sacrifices and the burdens which it can impose. Heroism is sometimes called for in

134   Cf. US National Conference of Catholic Bishops, Committee on Doctrine, "Moral Principles concerning Infants with Anencephaly," in *Origins* 10 (1996): 276.

135   John Paul II, Address to the participants in a meeting for obstetricians (January 26, 1980), n. 3: *AAS* 72 (1980), 86.

136   "To refuse to take part in committing an injustice is not only a moral duty; it is also a basic human right. Were this not so, the human person would be forced to perform an action intrinsically incompatible with human dignity, and in this way human freedom itself, the authentic meaning and purpose of which are found in its orientation to the true and the good, would be radically compromised. What is at stake therefore is an essential right which, precisely as such, should be acknowledged and protected by civil law. In this sense, the opportunity to refuse to take part in the phases of consultation, preparation and execution of these acts against life should be guaranteed to physicians, health care personnel, and directors of hospitals, clinics and convalescent facilities" (John Paul II, Encyclical Letter *Evangelium vitae*, n. 74: *AAS* 87 [1995], 488).

order to remain faithful to the requirements of the divine law. Therefore, we must emphasize that the path of true progress of the human person passes through this constant fidelity to a conscience maintained in uprightness and truth."[137]

Any attempt to delegitimize obedience to conscience, not only by means of penal sanctions but also by repercussions "on the legal, disciplinary, financial and professional plane,"[138] is to be condemned as a serious violation of human rights.

60.   Besides being a sign of professional integrity, a health care worker's earnestly motivated conscientious objection has the noble significance of *a social denunciation of a legal injustice* that is being perpetrated against innocent and defenseless lives.

Denunciation of legal injustices

61.   The seriousness of the sin of abortion[139] and the ease with which it is committed, with the approval of the law and of the current mindset, lead the Church to inflict the penalty of *excommunication* on any Christian who performs it or formally cooperates in it: "A person who actually procures an abortion incurs a *latae sententiae* excommunication."[140]

Decisive and credible witness

---

137   Congregation for the Doctrine of the Faith, *Declaration on Procured Abortion*, n. 24: *AAS* 66 (1974), 744.

138   John Paul II, Encyclical Letter *Evangelium vitae*, n. 74: *AAS* 87 (1995), 488.

139   "Procured abortion is *the deliberate and direct killing, by whatever means it is carried out, of a human being in the initial phase of his or her existence, extending from conception to birth*" (John Paul II, Encyclical Letter *Evangelium vitae*, n. 58: *AAS* 87 [1995], 467).

140   Cf. *CIC*, can. 1398. The expression "latae sententiae" means that it is not necessary for the excommunication to be pronounced by the authority in every single case. Anyone who procures abortion incurs it, by the mere fact of procuring it voluntarily and knowing that he incurs it. Cf. *CIC*, can. 1398, and *Code of Canons of Oriental Churches* (*CCEO*), can. 1450 §2; cf. also *CIC*, cann. 1323–1324.

The significance of excommunication is essentially preventive and pedagogical. It is a forceful call of the Church aimed at awakening dulled consciences, dissuading from an act that is absolutely incompatible with the demands of the Gospel, and inspiring unconditional fidelity to life. It is not possible to be in communion with the Church and to ignore the Gospel of life by committing abortion.

Defending and welcoming nascent human life is a decisive, credible witness that the Christian must give in every situation.

Duties toward aborted fetuses

62.   Health care workers have particular obligations toward aborted fetuses. An aborted fetus, if still alive, must be baptized, in so far as this is possible.[141]

An aborted fetus that is already dead deserves the respect owed to a human corpse, and if possible it should be given a suitable burial.[142]

Defending the right to life

Right to life with dignity

63. The right to life is the *right to live with human dignity*,[143] in other words, to be guaranteed this fundamental, original, and inalienable good, which is the root and prerequisite for every other right of the human person, and to have this good safeguarded.[144]

---

141   Cf. *CIC*, can. 871.

142   Cf. Congregation for the Doctrine of the Faith, Instruction *Donum vitae*, I, 4: *AAS* 80 (1988), 83.

143   Cf. John Paul II, Address to the Association of Italian Catholic Physicians (December 28, 1978), in *Insegnamenti* I (1978), 438; John Paul II, Address to participants in two congresses of medicine and surgery (October 27, 1980), n. 3: *AAS* 72 (1980), 1127; John Paul II, Address to a delegation from the association Food and Disarmament International (February 13, 1986), n. 3: *Insegnamenti* IX/1 (1986), 458.

144   Cf. Congregation for the Doctrine of the Faith, *Declaration on Euthanasia* (May 5, 1980), I: *AAS* 72 (1980), 544–545; John Paul II, Address to the World Medical Association (October 29, 1983), n. 2: *AAS* 76 (1984), 390.

"The human being is entitled to such rights, *in every phase of development,* from conception until natural death; and *in every condition,* whether healthy or sick, whole or handicapped, rich or poor."[145]

64. The right to life affects health care workers in two respects. First, they cannot claim to have a right of power over the life being cared for, because they have no such right and neither does the patient himself, so even the patient cannot grant it to them.[146]

The right to dispose of one's own life is not absolute: "No one ... can arbitrarily choose whether to live or die; the absolute master of such a decision is the Creator alone, in whom 'we live and move and have our being' (Acts 17:28)."[147]

No absolute right to dispose of one's own life

65.   In the second place, health care workers actively become the guarantors of this right: "the intrinsic purpose" of their profession "is the affirmation of the right of the human being to his life and his dignity."[148] They achieve it by assuming the corresponding duty of safeguarding health preventively and therapeutically[149] and improving (within the scope and with the means available to them) the quality of patients' lives and living conditions. In their endeavors, health care workers are guided and sustained by the law

Duty of safeguarding health

---

145 John Paul II, Apostolic Exhortation *Christifideles laici*, n. 38: *AAS* 81 (1989), 463.

146 "The doctor has no other rights or power over the patient than those which the latter gives him, explicitly or implicitly and tacitly. On his side, the patient cannot confer rights he does not possess" (Pius XII, Address to the members of the First International Congress on Histopathology of the Nervous System [September 14, 1952], n. 12: *AAS* 44 [1952], 782).

147 John Paul II, Encyclical Letter *Evangelium vitae*, n. 47: *AAS* 87 (1995), 453.

148 John Paul II, Address to the participants in a surgery congress (February 19, 1987), n. 2: *Insegnamenti* X/1 (1987), 374.

149 John Paul II, Address to the personnel of the new hospital Regina Margherita (December 20, 1981), n. 3: *Insegnamenti* IV/2 (1981), 1179.

of love, the source and model of which is the Son of God made man, who by dying gave life to the world.[150]

Subordination of labor union rights

66.   The fundamental and primary right of every human being to life, which more particularly entails the right to the protection of health, takes priority over the *labor union rights of health care workers*.

This implies that any just claim on the part of health care workers must be pursued while safeguarding the right of sick persons to the care that is owed them, because of the indispensability of that care. Therefore, in the case of a strike, medical and hospital services that are essential and urgent for the protection of health must be assured—even by means of appropriate legal measures.

Prevention

Primacy of prevention

67.   The protection of health commits health care workers first of all to the area of prevention. Preventing is better than treating, both because it spares the person the discomfort and suffering of illness, and also because it spares society the costs of treatment, which are not just economic.

Prevention and essential competency

68.   The *prevention proper to health care*, which includes administering particular pharmaceuticals, vaccinating, conducting tests or screenings to ascertain predispositions, and prescribing behaviors and habits aimed at avoiding the outbreak, spread, or worsening of diseases are essentially the competency of health care workers. It can be directed toward all the members of a society, to categories of persons, or to individuals, as may be the case with certain student health programs.

Prevention and vaccines

69.   From the perspective of preventing infectious diseases, the development of vaccines and their employment in the fight against such infections, through the obligatory

---

150   Cf. John Paul II, Encyclical Letter *Evangelium vitae*, n. 79: *AAS* 87 (1995), 491.

immunization of all the populations concerned, is undoubtedly a positive step.

The preparation of certain vaccines occasionally involves the use of *"biological material" of illicit origin*, for example, in the case of cell lines derived from deliberately aborted fetuses. The ethical problems here are essentially cooperation with evil and scandal, because of a grave disorder against the life and integrity belonging to every human being.[151] The duty remains for everyone to manifest disagreement with the use of biological material of illicit origin for the preparation of vaccines and to ask health care systems to make other types of vaccines available.[152]

No to the use of biological material of illicit origin

70.   In some cases, researchers utilize "biological material" of illicit origin that was not directly produced by those who make use of it, but acquired commercially; in these situations, one could invoke the criterion of independence, that is, the absence of any proximate connection to illicit practices. Nevertheless, the researchers, in their professional activity, have the duty to avoid scandal.

Hence "there is a duty to refuse to use such 'biological material' even when there is no close connection between the researcher and the actions of those who performed the artificial fertilization or the abortion, or when there was no prior agreement with the centers in which the artificial fertilization took place. This duty springs from the necessity to *remove oneself,* within the area of one's own research, *from a gravely unjust legal situation and to affirm with clarity the value of human life."*[153]

Duty to remove oneself from a gravely unjust legal situation

In this general context there are of course different levels of responsibility, so that serious reasons could

151   Cf. Congregation for the Doctrine of the Faith, Instruction *Dignitas personae*, n. 34: *AAS* 100 (2008), 882–883.

152   Cf. ibid., n. 35: *AAS* 100 (2008), 884; Pontifical Academy for Life, *Moral Reflections on Vaccines Prepared from Cells Derived from Aborted Human Fetuses* (Vatican City: 2005), n. 5.

153   Congregation for the Doctrine of the Faith, Instruction *Dignitas personae*, n. 35: *AAS* 100 (2008), 884.

be morally proportionate for the use of such "biological material" even though the duty remains for researchers to object to this situation and to try to make use of material not of illicit origin.[154]

Medical prevention and society

Prevention and preventive competency

71.   There is also a kind of *health care prevention in a broad sense,* in which the health care worker's activity is only one component of the preventive action carried out by society. This is the kind of prevention to be implemented in dealing with so-called social illnesses, such as drug dependence, alcoholism, and tobacco dependence.

This can be said all the more about the correct and appropriate prevention that health care workers are called to carry out, especially in dealing with the younger generations, with regard to *sexually transmitted diseases,* including the spread of the human immunodeficiency virus (HIV).

72.   Likewise, special attention should be paid to the *prevention of encumbrances for social groups of individuals*—such as adolescents, handicapped persons, and the elderly—and of health risks connected with contemporary living in relation to food, environment, workplace conditions, the home, sports, and such.

Concurrent action of all the forces in society

In these cases, preventive intervention is the primary and most effective remedy and sometimes the only one possible. It requires, however, the concurrent action of all the forces at work in society. Here prevention is more than a medical or health-care-related act. It is a matter of influencing the culture by recovering neglected values and providing the education that instills them, spreading a more measured and collaborative notion of life,

154 Cf. ibid.; Pontifical Academy for Life, *Moral Reflections on Vaccines Prepared from Cells Derived from Aborted Human Fetuses* (Vatican City: 2005), n. 5.

disseminating information about risky habits, and forming a political consensus for supportive legislation.

The real possibility of effective prevention is connected not only or primarily with the methods of implementation, but also with the motivations that sustain it and the extent of their dissemination and actualization in the culture.

Sickness

73.   Although it shares in the transcendent value of the person, bodily life, by its very nature, reflects the precariousness of the human condition. This is evident especially in sickness and suffering, which are experienced as a malaise of the whole person. "In fact, illness and suffering are not experiences which concern only man's physical substance, but man in his entirety and in his somatic-spiritual unity."[155] *Malaise of the whole person*

Sickness is more than a clinical, medically definable fact. It is always the condition of a human being, the sick person. Health care workers must approach patients with this *integrally human view* of sickness. In addition to the requisite technical or professional competence, they need to have an awareness of values and meanings that give purpose to sickness and to their own work, making every single clinical case a human encounter. *Corresponding approach of health care workers*

74.   Christians know by their faith that *sickness and suffering share in the saving power of the Cross of the Redeemer.* "Christ's redemption and his salvific grace reach the whole man in his human condition and therefore *Participation in saving power*

---

155   John Paul II, Motu Proprio *Dolentium hominum*, n. 2: *AAS* 77 (1985), 458. "Illness and suffering have always been among the gravest problems confronted in human life. In illness, man experiences his powerlessness, his limitations, and his finitude. Every illness can make us glimpse death" (*CCC*, n. 1500). "The mission of Jesus, with the many healings he performed, shows *God's great concern even for man's bodily life*" (John Paul II, Encyclical Letter *Evangelium vitae*, n. 47: *AAS* 87 [1995], 452).

reach also illness, suffering and death." [156] "On the Cross, the miracle of the serpent lifted up by Moses in the desert (Jn 3:14–15; cf. Num 21:8–9) is renewed and brought to full and definitive perfection. Today too, by looking upon the One who was pierced, every person whose life is threatened encounters the sure hope of finding freedom and redemption." [157]

"Down through the centuries and generations it has been seen that in suffering there is concealed a particular power that draws a person interiorly close to Christ, a special grace." [158] Sickness and suffering acquire an extraordinary spiritual fruitfulness when experienced in close union with the sufferings of Jesus, so that the sick person can say with the Apostle Paul, "In my flesh I complete what is lacking in Christ's afflictions for the sake of his body, that is, the Church" (Col 1:24). [159]

Threefold healthy attitude

This Christian reinterpretation can help the sick person develop a threefold healthy attitude toward his sickness: an *awareness* of its reality "without minimizing it or exaggerating it"; *acceptance* "not with a more or less blind resignation" but in the serene knowledge that "the Lord is able and wants to draw good from evil"; and an *offering* "made out of love for the Lord and for one's brethren." [160]

---

156 John Paul II, Motu Proprio *Dolentium hominum*, n. 2: *AAS* 77 (1985), 458.

157 John Paul II, Encyclical Letter *Evangelium vitae*, n. 50: *AAS* 87 (1995), 457.

158 John Paul II, Apostolic Letter *Salvifici doloris*, n. 26: *AAS* 76 (1984), 238.

159 "Even the sick are sent forth as laborers into the Lord's vineyard: the weight that wearies the body's members and dissipates the soul's serenity is far from dispensing a person from working in the vineyard. Instead the sick are called to live their human and Christian vocation and to participate in the growth of the Kingdom of God in a new and even more valuable manner" (John Paul II, Apostolic Exhortation *Christifideles laici*, n. 53: *AAS* 81 [1989], 499).

160 John Paul II, Address in Lourdes (August 15, 1983), n. 4: *Insegnamenti* VI/2 (1983), 242. "On the cross Christ took upon himself the whole weight of evil and took away the 'sin of the

75.   The family is always involved in some way with
the sick person.[161] Aid given to family members and their
cooperation with health care workers are valuable compo-
nents of health care.

Aid to family members

The health care worker, in dealing with the patient's
family, is called to provide, both individually and through
membership in associations, not only treatment but also
enlightenment, counsel, guidance, and support.[162]

Diagnosis

76.   Guided by this integrally human and properly
Christian understanding of sickness, the health care worker
seeks above all to discover the sickness and to analyze it in
the sick person: he formulates the *diagnosis* and the rela-
tive *prognosis*.

Diagnosis and prognosis with a human and Christian understanding of sickness

Indeed, a condition for any treatment is the precise
identification of the pathology in terms of its symptoms
and causes.

77.   In formulating a diagnosis, the health care worker
will take to heart the questions and anxieties of the patient,
and he must guard against the opposite extremes of *diagnostic abandonment* and *diagnostic obstinacy.*

Balance between diagnostic abandonment and diagnostic obstinacy

world' (Jn 1:29), of which illness is only a consequence. By his
passion and death on the cross Christ has given a new meaning to
suffering: it can henceforth configure us to him and unite us with
his redemptive Passion" (*CCC*, n. 1505).

161   "The family ... is the teacher of acceptance and solidarity: it is
within the family that education substantially draws upon relationships of solidarity; in the family one learns that the loss of health
is not a reason for discriminating against human life; the family
teaches us not to fall into individualism and to balance the 'I' with
the 'we.' It is there that 'taking care of one another' becomes a
foundation of human life and a moral attitude to foster, through
the values of commitment and solidarity" (Francis, Message to
participants in the General Assembly of the Pontifical Academy
for Life on the occasion of the twentieth anniversary of the institution [February 19, 2014]).

162   Cf. John Paul II, Apostolic Exhortation *Familiaris consortio*,
n. 75: *AAS* 74 (1982), 172–173.

In the first case, the patient is compelled to go from one specialist or one health care service to another, without finding the physician or the diagnostic center able and willing to treat his ailment. While the extreme specialization and compartmentalization of competencies and clinical departments guarantees professional expertise, it works to the detriment of the sick person when the national structure of health care delivery does not allow a careful, overall approach to his ailment.

In the second case, in contrast, there is a stubborn insistence on an excess of diagnostic tests, aimed at finding a sickness at all costs. One may be tempted, through laziness, profit-seeking, or self-aggrandizement, to diagnose a pathologic condition anyway and to medicalize problems that are not of a medical nature. This does not help the person grasp the exact nature of his own ailment or take the appropriate measures to overcome it.

Defensive medicine as a form of diagnostic obstinancy

A sort of obstinacy could become manifest in so-called *defensive medicine*, whereby health care workers modify their professional practice, adapting it solely to protect themselves from the legal consequences of their intervention.

For the benefit of health

78.   Ruling out such excesses, and guided by full respect for the dignity and integrity of the person, especially with regard to the use of invasive instrumental methods, diagnosis generally does not pose problems of an ethical nature. In itself it is ordered to therapy: it is an act that benefits health.

Particular problems are nonetheless posed by *predictive diagnostics*, because of the possible repercussions on the psychological level and forms of discrimination that may result from it.

Interventions on the genome

Prospects for genetic knowledge

79.   Ever more extensive knowledge about the *human genetic patrimony* (*genome*), the identification and mapping of genes with the possibility of transferring,

58

modifying, or replacing them, opens up previously unheard-of prospects for medicine and at the same time raises new and delicate ethical problems.

In a moral evaluation, strictly therapeutic interventions that aim to treat diseases resulting from genetic or chromosomal anomalies must be distinguished from manipulation that alters the human genetic patrimony.

Ethical distinction: therapeutic and manipulative alteratives

Gene therapy

80.   The application of genetic engineering techniques to human beings for therapeutic purposes, commonly referred to as *gene therapy*, is possible today at the level of the *somatic cells*, which make up tissues and organs. This type of gene therapy can be performed on a fetus, on an infant after birth, on a child, or on an adult.

In particular, "procedures used on somatic cells for strictly therapeutic purposes are in principle morally licit"[163] inasmuch as they aim to correct a genetic defect or cure a disease. In any case, it is nonetheless necessary to observe the principle that the subject being treated must not be exposed to risks to health and physical integrity that are excessive or disproportionate to the seriousness of the disease.[164] Furthermore, the informed consent of the patient or the patient's legal representative must be obtained.

Moral permissibility of gene therapy

Germ-line gene therapy, in contrast, at the present state of the research, is morally illicit, inasmuch as it is not yet possible to prevent the spread to the progeny of possible harm resulting from the intervention.[165]

---

163   Congregation for the Doctrine of the Faith, Instruction *Dignitas personae*, n. 26: *AAS* 100 (2008), 876.

164   Cf. John Paul II, Address to the World Medical Association (October 29, 1983), n. 6: *AAS* 76 (1984), 393. Cf. John Paul II, Address to the Pontifical Academy of Sciences (October 23, 1982), nn. 5, 6: *AAS* 76 (1983), 37, 38.

165   Cf. Congregation for the Doctrine of the Faith, Instruction *Dignitas personae*, n. 26: *AAS* 100 (2008), 877.

No to germ-line therapy

The application of this *therapy to the embryo* proves to be even more serious because, besides incurring the aforementioned risks, it needs to be carried out within the context of in vitro fertilization, with all the objections that such procedures entail. Given our present knowledge, therefore, germ-line gene therapy, in all its forms, is morally illicit.

No to manipulation for the purpose of improvement or enhancement

Supposing, then, that genetic engineering is applied to nontherapeutic ends for the purpose of using such techniques to perform *manipulations that presumably will improve and enhance one's genetic inheritance*, it becomes clear above all that "such manipulation would promote a eugenic mentality and would lead to indirect social stigma with regard to people who lack certain qualities, while privileging qualities that happen to be appreciated by a certain culture or society; such qualities do not constitute what is specifically human."[166] A judgment of moral liceity is incompatible with this ideological perspective, in which man claims to replace the Creator and which implies, among other things, an unjust domination of man over man.

Regenerative therapy

No to embryonic stem cells

81.   In the field of *regenerative medicine*, promising therapeutic applications have been made possible by the discovery of *stem cells*, both embryonic and non-embryonic.[167] In this respect, they should be considered in relation to the methods for obtaining stem cells.

---

166   Ibid., n. 27: *AAS* 100 (2008), 877.

167   Non-embryonic stem cells can come from (a) an aborted fetus; (b) fetal cells derived from the amniotic fluid before birth; (c) the placenta or the umbilical cord immediately after birth; or (d) the body of the infant or adult, and then they are called "somatic" cells. Furthermore, today there are also iPS cells (induced pluripotent stem cells). These are somatic cells—generally dermal fibroblasts—that have been genetically reprogrammed. They have characteristics similar to those of embryonic stem cells, but they are not obtained by the destruction of embryos.

These methods are ethically licit when the procurement of the stem cells does not cause serious damage to the donor.[168] They are, on the contrary, gravely illicit when they involve the procurement of stem cells from a living human embryo, because this inevitably causes its destruction.[169]

Also illicit is the harvesting of human fetal stem cells from a fetus that was killed by a procured abortion, if there is a direct relation between the act of abortion and the use of the stem cells.

As for the clinical or experimental use of stem cells obtained by means of licit procedures, the common criteria of professional medical standards must be observed, proceeding with great rigor and prudence, minimizing the possible risks to the patient, facilitating discussion in the scientific world, and offering adequate information about such innovative clinical applications.

82.   The production of embryonic stem cells is often connected with attempts at *human cloning*. Cloning has two basic goals: reproductive cloning, for the purpose of giving birth to a human being with particular, predefined characteristics, and so-called therapeutic or research cloning, for the purpose of obtaining stem cells.

No to human reproductive cloning

Reproductive human cloning is morally illicit, because it takes to an extreme the immorality inherent in techniques of artificial fertilization, attempting to "give rise to a new human being without a connection to the act of reciprocal self-giving between the spouses and, more radically, without any link to sexuality."[170]

---

168   Cf. Congregation for the Doctrine of the Faith, Instruction *Dignitas personae*, n. 32: *AAS* 100 (2008), 881.

169   Cf. ibid.

170   Ibid., n. 28: *AAS* 100 (2008), 879. Cf. Congregation for the Doctrine of the Faith, Instruction *Donum vitae*, II, B, 4: *AAS* 80 (1988), 90–92; John Paul II, Address to the World Medical Association (October 29, 1983), n. 6: *AAS* 76 (1984), 393.

The intention to predetermine the characteristics of a cloned individual would be for him a form of biological slavery and would be a serious offense against his human dignity and the fundamental equality of all human beings.[171]

No to so-called therapeutic cloning

So-called *therapeutic cloning* would be even more serious from the ethical point of view. Indeed, creating embryos with the intention of destroying them, even for the purpose of curing other sick persons, is altogether incompatible with respect for human life, even at the embryonic stage.[172]

Respect for nature

83.   The *manipulation of animal or plant cells for pharmaceutical purposes* raises no moral questions as long as it shows respect for nature, because "the natural environment is more than raw material to be manipulated at our pleasure; it is a wondrous work of the Creator, containing a 'grammar' which sets forth ends and criteria for its wise use, not its reckless exploitation."[173]

Treatment and rehabilitation

Performance of therapeutic and rehabilitative interventions

84.   Diagnosis is followed by *treatment* and *rehabilitation*, in other words, the performance of those interventions that permit, as much as possible, the recovery and the personal and social reintegration of the patient.

Treatment or therapy is a properly medical act, aimed at combating pathological conditions in their causes, manifestations, and complications. Rehabilitation, on the other hand, is a combination of medical, physiotherapeutic, and psychological measures together with functional training, aimed at restoring or improving the psychophysical efficiency of subjects who are in various ways impaired in their ability to integrate, to relate to others, and to be productive as workers.

171   Cf. Congregation for the Doctrine of the Faith, Instruction *Dignitas personae*, n. 29: *AAS* 100 (2008), 879.
172   Cf. ibid., n. 30: *AAS* 100 (2008), 879.
173   Benedict XVI, Encyclical Letter *Caritas in veritate*, n. 48: *AAS* 101 (2009), 685.

Treatment and rehabilitation are "directed not only to the good and the health of the body, but to the person as such who, in his body, is stricken by evil."[174] All treatment aimed at the holistic well-being of the person involves rehabilitative action as a way of *restoring the individual to himself, as much as possible*, through the reactivation and reappropriation of physical functions that had been impaired by sickness.

Holistic well-being of the person

85.   The sick person deserves treatments that are possible and from which he may derive some benefit.[175] Indeed, every human being has a primary right to what is necessary for the maintenance of his own health and therefore to *adequate health care*. Consequently, those who care for the sick have the duty to carry out their work with the utmost diligence and to provide any treatments considered necessary or useful.[176] This includes not only those that aim at a possible recovery, but also palliative treatments that relieve pain and ease an incurable condition. In this regard it is necessary to use special caution in resorting to treatments that lack documentation of scientific validity.

Right to adequate health care

86.   If recovery is impossible, the health care worker must never give up taking care of the person.[177] He is obliged to provide all *ordinary and proportionate care*.

Ordinary and proportionate care

Care is to be considered proportionate when there is *due proportion* between the means employed and therapeutic effectiveness. To verify this due proportion,

---

174 John Paul II, Motu Proprio *Dolentium hominum*, n. 2: *AAS* 77 (1985), 458. "Those whose lives are diminished or weakened deserve special respect. Sick or handicapped persons should be helped to lead lives as normal as possible" (*CCC*, n. 2276).

175 Cf. John Paul II, Address to the World Congress of Catholic Physicians (October 3, 1982), n. 3: *Insegnamenti* V/3 (1982), 673.

176 Cf. Congregation for the Doctrine of the Faith, *Declaration on Euthanasia*, IV: *AAS* 72 (1980), 550.

177 "Even when it cannot cure, science can and must care for and assist the patient" (John Paul II, Address to participants in a course on human pre-leukemias [November 15, 1985], n. 5: *AAS* 78 [1986], 361). Cf. John Paul II, Address to the Pontifical Academy of Sciences (October 21, 1985), n. 4: *AAS* 78 (1986), 314.

one must "make a correct judgment as to the means by studying the type of treatment to be used, its degree of complexity or risk, its cost, and the possibilities of using it, and comparing these elements with the result that can be expected, taking into account the state of the sick person and his or her physical and moral resources."[178]

Extraordinary means

Means are to be considered *extraordinary*, on the other hand, when they impose a heavy or excessive burden (whether material, physical, moral, or economic) on the patient, his family members, or the health care institution.[179] With all the more reason, treatments that have become futile must not be continued.

Ordinary means

The use of *ordinary means* of sustaining the patient's life is morally obligatory. On the other hand, extraordinary means may be declined with the patient's consent or upon his request, even if this hastens death. Physicians cannot be obliged to employ extraordinary means.[180]

Explanation of the principle of proportionality

87.   The principle of the *proportionality of treatment* just mentioned can be explained and applied as follows:

- "If there are no other sufficient remedies, it is permitted, with the patient's consent, to have recourse to the means provided by the most advanced medical techniques, even if these means are still at the experimental stage and are not without a certain risk."

- "It is also permitted, with the patient's consent, to interrupt these means, where the results fall short of expectations" because there is no longer due proportion between "the investment in instruments and personnel" and "the results foreseen" or because "the techniques applied impose on the patient strain or

---

178 Congregation for the Doctrine of the Faith, *Declaration on Euthanasia*, IV: *AAS* 72 (1980), 550.

179 Cf. Pius XII, Address to members of the Italian "Gregorio Mendel" Institute for Genetics on resuscitation and artificial respiration (November 24, 1957): *AAS* 49 (1957), 1027–1033.

180 Cf. Congregation for the Doctrine of the Faith, *Declaration on Euthanasia*, IV: *AAS* 72 (1980), 551.

suffering out of proportion with the benefits which he or she may gain from such techniques."

- "It is also permissible to make do with the normal means that medicine can offer. Therefore one cannot impose on anyone the obligation to have recourse to a technique which is already in use but which carries a risk or is burdensome. Such a refusal is not the equivalent of suicide." Instead it may simply indicate an "acceptance of the human condition, or a wish to avoid the application of a medical procedure disproportionate to the results that can be expected, or a desire not to impose excessive expense on the family or the community."[181]

88.   In the absence of other remedies, interventions involving the modification, mutilation, or removal of organs may be necessary to restore the person's health.

Principle of totality or therapeutic principle

The therapeutic manipulation of the human organism is legitimate in this case by virtue of the *principle of totality*[182] (which for this reason is also called the *therapeutic principle*), whereby "each particular organ is subordinate to the whole of the body and ought therefore to yield to it, in case of conflict."[183] Consequently, there is a right to sacrifice a particular organ if the preservation or the functioning of the organ causes considerable damage

---

181 Ibid.: *AAS* 72 (1980), 550–551.

182 "The principle of totality states that the part exists for the whole, and that consequently the good of the part remains subordinate to the good of the whole; that the whole is decisive for the part and can dispose of it in its own interest" [translated from French] (Pius XII, Address to members of the First International Congress of Histopathology of the Nervous System [September 14, 1952]: *AAS* 44 [1952], 787).

183 Pius XII, Address to participants in the Twenty-Sixth Congress of the Italian Urology Association (October 8, 1953): *AAS* 45 (1953), 674.

to the organism as a whole that is impossible to avoid otherwise.[184]

89.   Although physical life on the one hand manifests the person and takes on his value, so that it cannot be disposed of as a thing, on the other hand it is not exhaustive of the person's whole value and does not constitute his supreme good.[185]

Legitimate sacrifice of bodily life

This is why a part of the body can legitimately be disposed of for the well-being of the person. Likewise, physical life can be sacrificed or put at risk for a higher good, "such as God's glory, the salvation of souls or the service of one's brethren."[186] *Bodily life is a fundamental good*, the condition for all the others, but there are higher values for which it may be legitimate or even necessary to accept the danger of losing it.

Prescription and appropriate use of pharmaceuticals

Societal health care education on the excessive use of pharmaceuticals

90.   In countries with a universalized health care system, it is increasingly common to encounter an *excessive consumption of pharmaceuticals* in comparison with the health of the population; this is due to at least two factors.

---

184   Cf. Pius XII, Address to participants in the Twenty-Sixth Congress of the Italian Urology Association (October 8, 1953): *AAS* 45 (1953), 674–675. Cf. Pius XII, Address to members of the First International Congress of Histopathology of the Nervous System (September 14, 1952): *AAS* 44 (1952), 782–783. The principle of totality is applied at the level of the onset of the illness; only there is the relation of the part to the whole verified correctly. Bodily alterations cannot be legitimized for motivations that are not exclusively therapeutic. One may, however, legitimately intervene therapeutically in the case of psychological sufferings and spiritual discomfort that originate in a physical defect or lesion.

185   Cf. Congregation for the Doctrine of the Faith, Instruction *Donum vitae*, n. 3: *AAS* 80 (1988), 75.

186   Congregation for the Doctrine of the Faith, *Declaration on Euthanasia*, I: *AAS* 72 (1980), 545.

First is the issuance by physicians of prescriptions that are not particularly necessary, at the urgent request of the patient.

Second is a widespread recourse to pharmaceuticals not directly prescribed by the physician but taken as part of self-treatment, based on advice, information, or advertising furnished by means of social communication and by the internet. Particular attention should be paid to *pharmaceuticals of questionable preparation and origin*, distributed mainly through the internet, which do not guarantee efficacy and may be downright harmful to one's health.

Moreover, even when pharmaceuticals are correctly prescribed by the doctor, the person may tend to vary the dosage of his medications on his own, an attitude described as "non-adherence" to treatment, making it difficult if not impossible to evaluate their safety and therapeutic efficacy.

As part of their work of societal education about health care, health care workers must call due attention to the use of pharmaceuticals because of the social costs that they can entail, among other reasons.

Access to available medications and technologies

91.   Even today, in countries characterized by general well-being, and of course even more in developing countries—especially those characterized by political instability or scarce economic resources—there are still segments of the population for which access to health care services is not guaranteed, including access to life-saving medications and simple treatment options that technological progress has secured in modern medicine. As a result, medically treatable diseases continue to be endemic or are reappearing in countries that had eradicated them.

Extension to the whole population of the right to the preservation of health

Health care workers and their professional associations must become promoters of greater sensitivity in institutions, assisted-living facilities, and the health care industry, so that the *right to the preservation of health* may be extended to the whole population, albeit with the clear understanding that this right not only depends on health care facilities but is the result of economic, social and, more generally, cultural factors.

Those *responsible for health care activities* must also allow themselves to be uniquely and forcefully challenged by the awareness that "while the poor of the world continue knocking on the doors of the rich, the world of affluence runs the risk of no longer hearing those knocks, on account of a conscience that can no longer distinguish what is human."[187]

Sustainable health, pharmaceutical companies, rare or neglected diseases

Right of access to basic therapies

92.   The unequal distribution of economic resources, especially in underdeveloped and low-income countries, has important repercussions for *health care justice.*[188] In this context, although it cannot be denied that the scientific knowledge and research of *pharmaceutical companies*

187   Benedict XVI, Encyclical Letter *Caritas in veritate*, n. 75: *AAS* 101 (2009), 706. "The need to resolve the structural causes of poverty cannot be delayed, not only for the pragmatic reason of its urgency for the good order of society, but because society needs to be cured of a sickness which is weakening and frustrating it, and which can only lead to new crises. Welfare projects, which meet certain urgent needs, should be considered merely temporary responses. As long as the problems of the poor are not radically resolved by rejecting the absolute autonomy of markets and financial speculation and by attacking the structural causes of inequality, no solution will be found for the world's problems or, for that matter, to any problems. Inequality is the root of social ills" (Francis, Apostolic Exhortation *Evangelii gaudium*, n. 202). Cf. ibid., n. 203.

188   "We can no longer trust in the unseen forces and the invisible hand of the market. Growth in justice requires more than economic growth, while presupposing such growth: it requires decisions, programs, mechanisms and processes specifically geared to a better distribution of income, the creation of sources of employment and an integral promotion of the poor which goes beyond a simple welfare mentality" (Francis, Apostolic Exhortation *Evangelii gaudium*, n. 204).

have their own laws by which they must abide—for example, the protection of intellectual property and a fair profit to support innovation—ways must be found to combine these adequately with the right of access to basic or necessary treatments, or both, especially in underdeveloped countries,[189] and above all in the cases of so-called *rare*[190] and *neglected diseases*,[191] which are accompanied by the notion of *orphan drugs.*[192]

Health care strategies aimed at pursuing justice and the common good must be *economically and ethically sustainable.* Indeed, while they must safeguard the sustainability both of research and of health care systems, at the same time they ought to make available essential drugs in adequate quantities, in usable forms of guaranteed

Economically and ethically sustainable health care strategies

189 "It would also be advisable that the different pharmaceutical firms, laboratories at hospital centers and surgeries, as well as our contemporaries all together, be concerned with showing solidarity in the therapeutic context, to make access to treatment and urgently needed medicines available at all levels of society and in all countries, particularly to the poorest people" (Benedict XVI, Address to members of the International Congress of Catholic Pharmacists [October 29, 2007]: *AAS* 99 [2007], 932).

190 A disease is described as "rare" when its prevalence, understood as the number of cases occurring in a given population, does not surpass an established threshold. In the European Union the threshold is set at 0.05 percent of the population, in other words, five cases for every ten thousand persons.

191 According to the most recent definition, the term "neglected diseases" means those diseases that do not receive the attention that they deserve; these are, specifically, parasitic diseases connected with poverty, chiefly infectious "tropical" diseases, except for malaria, tuberculosis, the HIV/AIDS virus, potentially epidemic or pandemic diseases (e.g., forms of influenza), and diseases that are preventable by vaccination (e.g., measles, poliomyelitis).

192 An "orphan" drug is a product that is potentially useful in treating a rare disease but does not have a large enough market to recover the cost of developing it. It is called an orphan drug because there is a lack of interest among pharmaceutical companies in investing in a drug designed for so few patients, even though the drug would address a public health need.

quality, along with correct information, and at costs that are affordable by individuals and communities.

Pain relief treatments

Biological function of pain

93.   Pain has a biological function, because it is a symptom of a pathological situation and "helps the physical and the psychic in man to concur in reaction" to it.[193] Nevertheless, it calls on medicine for *palliative treatment*: a human person in fact has the "right to dominate the forces of nature, to use them in his service, and thus to make profitable all the resources that it offers him to avoid or remove the physical pain."[194]

Harmful effects on psycho-physical integrity

94.   "In the long run pain is an obstacle to the attainment of higher goods and interests."[195] It can cause harmful effects to the psychophysical integrity of the person. Suffering that is too intense can diminish or impede the mastery exercised by the spirit. "The suppression of pain, instead, brings organic and psychic relief, making prayer easier and enabling one to give oneself more generously."[196] The use of painkillers, "by directly acting on the more aggressive and disturbing effects of pain, gives the person more control, so that suffering becomes a more human experience."[197]

Penitential and salvific meaning

95.   For the Christian, *pain can take on a noble penitential and salvific meaning.* "It is in fact a sharing in Christ's passion and a union with the redeeming sacrifice which He offered in obedience to the Father's will. Therefore, one

---

193   John Paul II, Address to participants in the Congress of the Italian Association of Anesthesiology (October 4, 1984), n. 2: *AAS* 77 (1985), 133.

194   Pius XII, Address to an international assembly of physicians and surgeons, "En réponse à trois questions religieuses et morales concernant l'analgésie" (February 24, 1957): *AAS* 49 (1957), 135.

195   Ibid.: *AAS* 49 (1957), 136.

196   Ibid.: *AAS* 49 (1957), 144.

197   John Paul II, Address to participants in the Congress of the Italian Association of Anesthesiology (October 4, 1984), n. 3: *AAS* 77 (1985), 135.

must not be surprised if some Christians prefer to moderate their use of painkillers in order to accept voluntarily at least a part of their sufferings and thus associate themselves in a conscious way with the sufferings of Christ crucified."[198]

The free acceptance of pain for Christian motives must not suggest that we ought not to intervene to assuage it. On the contrary, professional duty as well as Christian charity itself demand that efforts be made to alleviate suffering, and call for medical research in this field.

Informed consent of the patient

96.   The health care worker can intervene if he has previously obtained *the patient's consent, implicitly* (when the medical acts are routine and involve no particular risks) or *explicitly* (in documentable form when the treatments involve risks). Indeed, the health care worker has no separate or independent right in dealing with the patient. In general, he can act only if the patient authorizes it explicitly or implicitly (directly or indirectly). Without this authorization, the health care worker is arrogating an arbitrary power to himself.

The relationship between the health care worker and the patient is a *human relationship of dialogue*, and not a subject–object relation. The patient "is not an anonymous individual" on whom medical expertise is practiced, but "a responsible person, who should be called upon to share in the improvement of his health and in becoming cured. He should be enabled to choose personally, and not be made to submit to the decisions and choices of others."[199]

Medical relationship characterized by dialogue

In order for the patient to make a choice that is fully informed and free, he must have as complete a view as possible of his ailment and the possible treatments, with the risks, difficulties and consequences that they

Right to informed consent

198   Congregation for the Doctrine of the Faith, *Declaration on Euthanasia*, III: *AAS* 72 (1980), 547.

199   John Paul II, Address to the World Congress of Catholic Physicians (October 3, 1982), n. 4: *Insegnamenti* V/3 (1982), 673.

involve.[200] This means that the patient's *informed consent* must be requested.

97.	*Consent may be presumed* in a case where the health care worker is called to intervene on a patient who is momentarily or permanently incapable of understanding and deciding, so as to save the patient from a situation of serious danger to his life or his health, with treatments appropriate to the risks and the urgency.

In this case, the duty to intervene is by reason of the principle of responsibility in care, which obliges the health care worker to take charge of the patient's life and health unless the patient, previous to his state of incapacity, expressed to the health care worker a legitimate and explicit dissent or disagreement about particular treatments.

Legal
representative
and
involvement
of relatives

98.	In a case where the patient is not capable of understanding the necessary information about his state of health, the prognosis, and the treatments and there is no urgent need to intervene, the health care worker must communicate the information about the patient's state of health to the legal representative and request consent for the medical treatments from the person who is legally authorized to provide it.[201] If the latter cannot be identified, the health care worker must be proactive and point out the need for one to be named.

When the patient authorizes it, his relatives can be informed about his state of health and his treatments and be involved in these decisions.

Biomedical research and experimentation

Scientific
progress and
experimental
research

99.	In the context of prevention, diagnosis and cure, medical acts—the purpose of which is to achieve increasingly effective results for the benefit of the patient's

200	Cf. John Paul II, Address to participants in the Congress of Medicine and Surgery (October 27, 1980), n. 5: *AAS* 72 (1980), 1127–1128.

201	Cf. *CCC*, n. 2278.

health—are by their very nature open to innovative treatments. The latter are the result of constant and gradual research and experimentation, with the purpose of identifying new and better treatment solutions, scientifically validating them, and making them available to patients.[202]

Proceeding by way of research and experimentation is the law of any applied science: scientific progress is structurally connected with it. The biomedical sciences and their development are not exempt from this law.

Biomedical research, however, is necessarily conducted with human subjects who are precious and fragile.

Human persons—both so-called healthy volunteers and sick people—can be involved and voluntarily offer their own contribution to medical research, provided that all necessary precautions are taken to avoid risks to their psychological and physical integrity, to avoid worsening their health, and to respect their dignity. For this reason, the biomedical sciences do not have the same investigational freedom enjoyed by the sciences that apply to things.[203] "Research or experimentation on the human being cannot legitimate acts that are in themselves contrary to the dignity of persons and to the moral law. The subjects' potential consent does not justify such acts. Experimentation on human beings is not morally legitimate if it exposes the subject's life or physical and psychological integrity to disproportionate or avoidable risks. Experimentation on human beings does not conform to the dignity of the person if it takes place without the informed consent of the subject or those who legitimately speak for him."[204]

The collaboration of persons as subjects in biomedical research, based on a *free and responsible decision*

Biomedical research as an expression of solidarity and charity

202 "Scientific, medical, or psychological experiments on human individuals or groups can contribute to healing the sick and the advancement of public health" (*CCC*, n. 2292).
203 Cf. *CCC*, nn. 2293–2294.
204 Ibid., n. 2295.

73

shared with the medical researcher, is a particular expression of solidarity and charity.

Immorality of research contrary to the true good of the person

100.   The ethical norms of research require that it be directed toward promoting human well-being. All research contrary to the true good of the person is immoral;[205] investing efforts and resources in it is contrary to the human purpose of science and scientific progress.[206]

In the *experimentation* phase, or the testing of a research study's hypotheses on human beings, the good of the person—protected by ethical norms—demands respect for preconditions connected essentially with consent and risk.

Risk factor and degree of danger

101.   First is the *risk factor*. In itself all experimentation involves some risks. However, "there is a degree of danger that morality cannot allow."[207] There is a threshold

205   "The Church respects and supports scientific research when it has a genuinely humanist orientation, avoiding any form of instrumentalization or destruction of the human being and keeping itself free from the slavery of political and economic interests. In presenting the moral orientations dictated by natural reason, the Church is convinced that she offers a precious service to scientific research, doing her utmost for the true good of the human person. In this perspective, she recalls that, not only the aims, but also the methods and means of research must always respect the dignity of every human being, at every stage of his development and in every phase of experimentation" (John Paul II, Address to members of the Pontifical Academy for Life [February 24, 2003], n. 4: *AAS* 95 [2003], 590–591).

206   Cf. John Paul II, Address to participants in a conference promoted by the Pontifical Commission for Pastoral Assistance to Health Care Workers (November 12, 1987), n. 4: *AAS* 80 (1988), 644. "Mention should also be made here of theories which misuse scientific research about the human person. Arguing from the great variety of customs, behavior patterns and institutions present in humanity, these theories end up, if not with an outright denial of universal human values, at least with a relativistic conception of morality" (John Paul II, Encyclical Letter *Veritatis splendor*, n. 33: *AAS* 85 [1993], 1160).

207   Pius XII, Address to members of the First International Congress of Histopathology of the Nervous System (September 14, 1952): *AAS* 44 (1952), 788.

beyond which the risk becomes humanly unacceptable. This threshold is defined by the inviolable good of the person, which forbids all concerned "to endanger his life, his equilibrium, his health, or to aggravate his illness."[208]

The properly documented *provision of adequate information and verification of understanding*, for the purposes of obtaining free and cognizant consent from the persons involved, are always a necessary and indispensable element for *ethical experimentation*, both when the objectives are strictly for scientific knowledge and when these are connected with additional objectives involving therapeutic potential.

Information and understanding for the purpose of ethical experimentation

Minors or adults who are legally not capable of understanding and making decisions can also be involved in clinical experimentation, provided that, subject to the criteria of scientific validity, their involvement is justified by a proportionality between the reasonably foreseeable risks and benefits for the minor or incapacitated subjects. Experimentation that is not expected to provide direct benefits for the minor or incapacitated subjects, but only for other persons in similar conditions (in terms of age, type of illness, and other characteristics), can be ethically justified when it is not possible to obtain the same results through experiments on adult, competent subjects and the risks and burdens are minimal. In both cases, informed consent must be requested of the parents or the legal representative in accordance with the laws of each particular country.

Involvement of minors or adults who are not legally capable of understanding and making decisions

102.   Experimentation cannot be initiated and continued unless all precautions have been taken to avoid foreseeable risks and to reduce the consequences of adverse outcomes.

To obtain these assurances, a phase of basic *preclinical research* is necessary, which must provide the fullest documentation and the surest guarantees about

Preclinical research

---

208   John Paul II, Address to an international conference on pharmacy (October 24, 1986), n. 4: *Insegnamenti* IX/2 (1986), 1183.; cf. John Paul II, Address to participants in a congress on surgery (February 19, 1987), n. 4: *Insegnamenti* X/1 (1987), 376; *CCC*, n. 2295.

pharmacological toxicology and operating techniques.[209] To this end, if useful and necessary, experimentation with new drugs or new techniques cannot exclude the *use of animals* before going on to human subjects. "It is certain that animals are at the service of man and can hence be the object of experimentation. Nevertheless, they must be treated as creatures of God which are destined to serve man's good, but not to be abused by him."[210] It follows that all experimentation "should be carried out with consideration for the animal, without causing it useless suffering."[211]

Principle of proportionate risk

Once these guarantees are met, in the *clinical phase* human experimentation must abide by the *principle of proportionate risk*, that is, of a due proportion between foreseeable harms and benefits.

In such an important field it is reasonable to take into consideration the opinions of competent persons with sound moral qualities. Today this is typically achieved through the opinion of *ethics committees* for research. It is the responsibility of Catholic health care workers (physicians, pharmacists, nurses, chaplains, experts in health care law, etc.) to be present on such panels to examine the value and the scientific validity of the experimental research plan and to ensure that the rights and dignity of all those who participate in biomedical research are safeguarded.

Ethics committees

Consent of the subject

103.   Second, *the consent of the subject* is needed. He "must be informed of the experimentation, of its purpose and any risks it involves, so that he may give or refuse his

---

209 Cf. John Paul II, Address to participants in two congresses on medicine and surgery (October 27, 1980), nn. 5, 6: *AAS* 72 (1980), 1127–1129; John Paul II, Address to participants in a course on human preleukemias (November 15, 1985), n. 5: *AAS* 78 (1986), 361–362.

210 John Paul II, Address to members of the Pontifical Academy of Sciences (October 23, 1982), n. 4: *AAS* 75 (1983), 37. "Hence the diminution of experimentation on animals, which has progressively been made ever less necessary, corresponds to the plan and well-being of all creation" (ibid.).

211 John Paul II, Address to an international conference on pharmacy (October 24, 1986), n. 4: *Insegnamenti* IX/2 (1986), 1183.

consent in full awareness and freedom. The doctor, in fact, has only that power and those rights over the patient which the patient himself confers to him."[212]

It is necessary to distinguish between experimentation on a sick person for therapeutic purposes and on a healthy or sick person for the purpose of scientific knowledge or for the benefit of other subjects. The same guarantees apply to pharmacological and surgical research and to innovative research involving gene therapy or the use of stem cells.

Experimentation for therapeutic and scientific purposes

104.   In *experimentation on a sick person for therapeutic purposes*, due proportion must be attained by comparing the conditions of the sick person with the possible clinical benefits of the experimental drugs or methods.

Criteria regarding the sick person

The evaluation of the risks must be done in advance by the researcher and by the ethics committee, and this is a fundamental aspect of the ethical justification for any clinical experimentation.

For this evaluation, the already-stated principle applies: "If there are no other sufficient remedies, it is permitted, with the patient's consent, to have recourse to the means provided by the most advanced medical techniques, even if these means are still at the experimental stage and are not without a certain risk. By accepting them, the patient can even show generosity in the service of humanity."[213]

Permissibility of recourse to means not yet without a certain risk

212   John Paul II, Address to participants in two congresses on medicine and surgery (October 27, 1980), n. 5: *AAS* 72 (1980), 1127–1128.

213   Congregation for the Doctrine of the Faith, *Declaration on Euthanasia*, IV: *AAS* 72 (1980), 550. "In doubtful cases, when means already known have failed, it may happen that a new method still insufficiently tried offers, together with very dangerous elements, appreciable chances of success. If the patient gives his consent, the use of the procedure in question is licit" (Pius XII, Address to members of the First International Congress of Histopathology of the Nervous System [September 14, 1952]: *AAS* 44 [1952], 788).

In clinical cases in which there are no other proven treatments, one may proceed, with the consent of the patient or of his legal representative and the approval of the ethics committee, to the application of treatments that are still in the experimental phase, even if they present a high percentage of risk.[214]

Presumed consent for experimentation in emergency situation

In clinical experimentation, *presumed consent* can be taken into consideration only in the case of an experimental procedure to be carried out in an urgent or emergency situation on patients who are not capable of understanding and deciding and are suffering from a pathology for which the experimental procedure is the sole possibility for treatment and the experimentation has been approved previously by an ethics committee. Later the patient, if he regains competence (or his legal representative if the patient's incapacity persists), must be informed about the experimentation and either confirm his participation or not (deferred consent).

Experimentation on a healthy person, and the principle of solidarity

105.   *Clinical experimentation* can be carried out also *on a healthy person* who voluntarily offers himself "to contribute by his initiative to the progress of medicine and, in that way, to the good of the community." This is legitimized by human and Christian solidarity, which justifies the gesture and gives it meaning and value: "To give something of oneself, within the limits laid down by the moral norm, may constitute a highly meritorious witness of charity and an occasion of spiritual growth so significant as to be able to compensate for the risk of a slight physical disability."[215]

In any case, it is always necessary to interrupt the experimentation if intermediate evaluations indicate an excessive risk or a clear lack of benefit.

---

214 Cf. Pius XII, Address to participants in the Eighth Assembly of the World Medical Association (September 30, 1954): *AAS* 46 (1954), 591–592.

215 John Paul II, Address to participants in two congresses on medicine and surgery (October 27, 1980), n. 5: *AAS* 72 (1980), 1128.

106.　Since it must be acknowledged that an individual human being in the prenatal stage has the dignity of a human person, *research and experimentation on human embryos and fetuses* must be subject to the ethical norms that apply to a child who is already born and to any human subject.

　　In particular, research through the observation of a given phenomenon *during pregnancy* can be allowed only when "there is a moral certainty of not causing harm to the life or integrity of the unborn child and the mother, and on condition that the parents have given their free and informed consent to the procedure."[216]

　　Experimentation involving new interventions, on the other hand, is possible only when valid scientific prerequisites are in place and only for clearly therapeutic purposes, in the absence of other possible treatments. On the other hand, "no objective, even though noble in itself, such as a foreseeable advantage to science, to other human beings, or to society, can in any way justify experimentation on living human embryos or fetuses, whether viable or not, either inside or outside the mother's womb. The informed consent ordinarily required for clinical experimentation on adults cannot be granted by the parents, who may not freely dispose of the physical integrity or life of the unborn child. Moreover, experimentation on embryos and fetuses always involves risk, and indeed in most cases it involves the certain expectation of harm to their physical integrity or even their death. To use human embryos or fetuses as the object or instrument of experimentation constitutes a crime against their dignity as human beings." In particular, "the practice of keeping alive human embryos in vivo or in vitro for experimental or commercial purposes is totally opposed to human dignity."[217]

216　Congregation for the Doctrine of the Faith, Instruction *Donum vitae*, I, 4: *AAS* 80 (1988), 81.

217　Ibid.: *AAS* 80 (1988), 82. "I condemn, in the most explicit and formal way, experimental manipulations of the human embryo, since the human being, from conception to death, cannot be

Experimentation on vulnerable persons

107. In clinical experimentation, moreover, special attention must be given to the involvement of *persons* who may be *vulnerable* because of dependence (students, prisoners, military service personnel), social insecurity or poverty (the homeless, the unemployed, immigrants), or lack of education, which could make it difficult to obtain valid informed consent.

In emerging and developing countries, experimentation should have first and foremost clinical and scientific objectives that directly and specifically concern the local populations involved. The scientific and ethical criteria used to evaluate and conduct the experiments in emerging and developing countries must be the same as those used for experimentation conducted in developed countries.

Experiments in emerging and developing countries must be conducted with respect to local traditions and cultures and should be approved in advance by either a national ethics committee of the sponsoring country or by the local ethics committee.

Experimentation on women with childbearing potential

108. In *clinical experiments*, especially those dealing with serious pathologies for which there is no proven treatment, experimental treatments could also involve women *of childbearing potential* and men, with possible risks in the case of pregnancy. The patients must be made aware of these risks before deciding to participate in the experimentation, knowing that they must avoid starting a pregnancy until the harmful effects of the treatment have ended.

The physician or the commercial sponsor of the experimental research cannot request the use of contraceptive or, worse still, abortive methods as a condition for participating in the experimentation.

exploited for any purpose whatsoever" (John Paul II, Address to members of the Pontifical Academy of Sciences [October 23, 1982], n. 4: *AAS* 75 [1983], 37).

Organ and tissue donation and transplantation

109.   The progress and spread of transplantation medicine today allows the treatment and recovery of many patients with serious ailments who until recently could expect only death or at best a painful, restricted life.[218]

The donation and transplantation of organs are significant expressions of *service to life* and of the *solidarity* that binds human beings together, and they are "a peculiar form of witness to charity."[219] For these reasons, they have a moral value that legitimizes their use in medical practice.

Moral value of organ donation and transplantation

110.   The medical intervention of transplantation is "inseparable from a human act of donation."[220] In donating organs, indeed, the donor generously and freely consents to their removal.

When an organ is *procured from a living donor*, the *consent* must be given personally by a subject capable of expressing it.[221] Special attention should be given to subjects in particularly vulnerable conditions.

Consent for procurement from a living donor

When an organ is *procured from a cadaver*, the consent must have been expressed somehow during the donor's lifetime or made by someone who can legally represent him. Biomedical progress "has made it possible for people to project beyond death their vocation to love"; this should lead persons to "offer in life a part of one's body, an offering which will become effective only after

Consent for procurement from a cadaver

---

218   Cf. John Paul II, Address to participants in the First International Congress of the Society for Organ Sharing (June 20, 1991), n. 1: *Insegnamenti* XIV/1 (1991), 1710.

219   Benedict XVI, Address to participants in the international congress organized by the Pontifical Academy for Life (November 7, 2008): *AAS* 100 (2008), 802.

220   John Paul II, Address to participants in the First International Congress of the Society for Organ Sharing (June 20, 1991), n. 3: *Insegnamenti* XIV/1 (1991), 1711.

221   Cf. *CCC*, n. 2296.

death." This is "an act of *great love*, the love which gives life to others."[222]

111.   As part of this sacrificial "economy" of love, the medical act of transplantation itself, and even the simple transfusion of blood, "must not be separated from the donor's act of self-giving, from the love that gives life."[223]

Mediating character of medical interventions

Here the health care worker "becomes the mediator of something especially significant, the gift of self which one person has made even after death so that another might live."[224] "The right road to follow, until science is able to discover other new forms and more advanced therapies, must be the formation and the spreading of a culture of solidarity that is open to all and does not exclude anyone."[225]

Transplants involving the same person

112.   *Autograft transplants*, in which the removal and the transplant are performed on the same person, are legitimized by the principle of totality, by virtue of which it is

---

222 John Paul II, Address to participants in the First International Congress of the Society for Organ Sharing (June 20, 1991), n. 4: *Insegnamenti* XIV/1 (1991), 1712; cf. *CCC*, n. 2301.

223 Ibid., n. 5: *Insegnamenti* XIV/1 (1991), 1713.

224 Ibid. "The difficulty of the operation, the need to act swiftly, the need for complete concentration on the task, should not make the physician lose sight of the mystery of love involved in what he is doing." "The different commandments of the Decalogue are really only so many reflections of the one commandment about the good of the person, at the level of the many different goods which characterize his identity as a spiritual and bodily being in relationship with God, with his neighbor and with the material world" (John Paul II, Encyclical Letter *Veritatis splendor*, n. 13: *AAS* 85 [1993], 1143–1144).

225 Benedict XVI, Address to participants in the international congress organized by the Pontifical Academy for Life (November 7, 2008): *AAS* 100 (2008), 804. "A medical transplantation corresponds to an ethic of donation that demands on the part of all the commitment to invest every possible effort in formation and information, to make the conscience ever more sensitive to an issue that directly touches the life of many people. Therefore it will be necessary to reject prejudices and misunderstandings, widespread indifference and fear to substitute [i.e., so as to replace] them with certainty and guarantees in order to permit an ever more heightened and diffuse awareness of the great gift of life in everyone" (ibid.).

possible to dispose of one part for the integral good of the organism.

One particular form of autograft transplantation involves *ovarian germinal cells* removed from a subject before very aggressive chemotherapy or radiation therapy that is potentially harmful for her future fertility. The preservation and orthotopic transfer of autologous ovarian tissue are acceptable in principle.

Autograph transplantation of ovarian germinal cells

113.   *Homograft transplants*, in which the removal is performed on an individual of the same species as the recipient, are legitimized by the principle of solidarity that unites human beings. "With the advent of organ transplantation, which began with blood transfusions, man has found a way to give of himself, of his blood and of his body, so that others may continue to live. Thanks to science, and to the professional training and commitment of doctors and health care workers, new and wonderful challenges are presented. We are challenged to love our neighbor in new ways; in evangelical terms, to love 'to the end' (cf. Jn 13:1), yet within certain limits which cannot be exceeded, limits laid down by human nature itself."[226]

Transplantation from one person to another

Explanation of the principle of solidarity

114.   Organs can be procured from *a living donor* or *from a cadaver* in homograft transplants. In the first case, the removal is lawful provided that "the physical and psychological dangers and risks incurred by the donor are proportionate to the good sought for the recipient. It is morally inadmissible directly to bring about the disabling mutilation or death of a human being, even in order to delay the death of other persons."[227]

Criteria for permissibility of organ procurement from a living donor or from a cadaver

In the second case, we are no longer dealing with a living person but with a cadaver. It should still be respected as a human cadaver, but it no longer has the dignity of a

226   John Paul II, Address to participants in the First International Congress of the Society for Organ Sharing (June 20, 1991), n. 2: *Insegnamenti* XIV/1 (1991), 1711.

227   *CCC*, n. 2296.

subject and a living person's value as an end. "A corpse is no longer, in the proper sense of the term, a subject of rights, because it is deprived of personality, which alone can be the subject of rights." Hence, "to put it to useful purposes, morally blameless and even noble," is a decision "not be condemned but to be positively justified."[228] This consignment, however, requires either the consent of the deceased person, given before death, or else the non-opposition of his legitimate representatives. The free donation of organs after death is permissible.[229]

Certainty following diagnosis
It is necessary, though, to be certain that one is dealing with a cadaver, so as to make sure that the removal of organs does not cause or even merely anticipate death. The removal of organs from a cadaver is legitimate following a sure diagnosis of the donor's death. Hence the duty "to take care that a 'corpse' shall not be considered and treated as such until death has been sufficiently proved."[230]

Determination of death

115.   The removal of vital organs from a cadaver poses the problem of diagnosing death with certainty in a new way.

Man perceives death as a decomposition, dissolution, or breaking apart,[231] "consisting in the total disintegration of that unitary and integrated whole that is

---

228   Pius XII, Address to delegates of the Italian Association of Cornea Donors and the Italian Union for the Blind (May 14, 1956): *AAS* 48 (1956), 462–464.

229   Cf. *CCC*, n. 2301.

230   Pius XII, Address to delegates of the Italian Association of Cornea Donors and the Italian Union for the Blind (May 14, 1956): *AAS* 48 (1956), 466–467.

231   Cf. Vatican Council II, Pastoral Constitution *Gaudium et spes*, n. 18; John Paul II, Apostolic Letter *Salvifici doloris*, n. 15: *AAS* 76 (1984), 216; Vatican Council II, Address to participants in the working group on the determination of brain death (December 14, 1989), n. 4: *AAS* 82 (1990), 768.

the personal self."[232] "This destruction does not of course affect the entire human being. Christian faith—and it is not alone here—affirms the continuation of man's spiritual principle beyond death."[233]

"The death of the person ... is an event which no scientific technique or empirical method can identify directly. Yet human experience shows that once death occurs, certain biological signs inevitably follow, which medicine has learnt to recognize with increasing precision. In this sense, the 'criteria' for ascertaining death used by medicine today should not be understood as the technical-scientific determination of the *exact moment* of a person's death, but as a scientifically secure means of identifying the biological signs that a person has indeed died."[234]

Criteria for determination of death

From the biomedical perspective, *death consists in the total loss of integration of that unified whole which is the human organism.* The medical observation and interpretation of the signs of this disintegration do not pertain to morality but to science. It is properly up to medicine to determine as precisely as possible the *clinical signs of death.* Once this medical determination has been made, it becomes possible to address the moral questions and conflicts raised by the new technologies and treatment options in light of this assessment.

Clinical signs of death

232 John Paul II, Address to participants in an international congress on organ transplants (August 29, 2000), n. 4: *AAS* 92 (2000), 823–824.

233 John Paul II, Address to participants in the working group on the determination of brain death (December 14, 1989), n. 4: *AAS* 82 (1990), 769. "The unity of soul and body is so profound that one has to consider the soul to be the 'form' of the body: i.e., it is because of its spiritual soul that the body made of matter becomes a living, human body; spirit and matter, in man, are not two natures united, but rather their union forms a single nature" (*CCC*, n. 365). "The Church teaches that every spiritual soul is created immediately by God—it is not 'produced' by the parents—and also that it is immortal: it does not perish when it separates from the body at death, and it will be reunited with the body at the final Resurrection" (*CCC*, n. 366).

234 John Paul II, Address to participants in an international congress on organ transplants (August 29, 2000), n. 4: *AAS* 92 (2000), 824.

116.   "It is a well-known fact that for some time certain scientific approaches to ascertaining death have shifted the emphasis from the traditional cardiorespiratory signs to the so-called *neurological criterion*. Specifically, this consists in establishing, according to clearly determined parameters commonly held by the international scientific community, the complete and irreversible cessation of all brain activity (in the cerebrum, cerebellum, and brain stem). This is then considered the sign that the individual organism has lost its integrative capacity.

Encephalic signs and cardio-respiratory signs

"With regard to the parameters used today for ascertaining death—whether the 'encephalic' signs or the more traditional cardiorespiratory signs—the Church does not make technical decisions. She limits herself to the Gospel duty of comparing the data offered by medical science with the Christian understanding of the unity of the person, bringing out the similarities and the possible conflicts capable of endangering respect for human dignity."[235]

Legitimacy of the neurological criterion

If the scientific data do offer grounds for stating that the criterion of whole-brain death and the related signs indicate with surety that the unity of the organism has been lost irreversibly, then it can be declared that the *neurological criterion*, "if rigorously applied, does not seem to conflict with the essential elements of a sound anthropology. Therefore, a health worker professionally responsible for ascertaining death can use these criteria in each individual case as the basis for arriving at that degree of assurance in ethical judgment which moral teaching describes as 'moral certainty.' This moral certainty is considered the necessary and sufficient basis for an ethically correct course of action. Only where such certainty exists, and where informed consent has already been given by the donor or the donor's legitimate representatives, is it morally right to initiate the technical procedures required for the removal of organs for transplant."[236]

235   Ibid., n. 5: *AAS* 92 (2000), 824.
236   Ibid.

"In an area such as this, in fact, there cannot be the slightest suspicion of arbitrariness, and where certainty has not been attained, the principle of precaution must prevail. This is why it is useful to promote research and interdisciplinary reflection to place public opinion before the most transparent truth on the anthropological, social, ethical, and juridical implications of the practice of transplantation."[237]

Principle of precaution must prevail

The removal of organs from pediatric donors

117.   Particular care must be used in the *procurement of organs from pediatric donors* because of the need to apply to the child specifically tailored parameters for determining death and because of the delicate psychological situation of the parents, who are called upon to give consent for the removal. The need for organs from pediatric donors can in no way justify the omission of the proper verification of the clinical signs for the determination of death of a pediatric patient.

Proper verification of clinical signs

Xenotransplants

118.   There is an ongoing discussion about the possibility, which is still entirely experimental, of solving the problem of obtaining organs for human transplantation by resorting to the use of xenograft transplants, that is, *the transplantation of organs and tissues derived from animals.* "For a xenotransplant to be licit, the transplanted organ must not impair the integrity of the psychological or genetic identity of the person receiving it; and there must also be a proven biological possibility that the transplant will be successful and will not expose the recipient to

Criteria for permissibility

---

237 Benedict XVI, Address to participants in the international congress organized by the Pontifical Academy for Life (November 7, 2008): *AAS* 100 (2008), 804.

inordinate risk."[238] Moreover, it is necessary to respect the animals involved in these procedures by observing certain conditions: "Unnecessary animal suffering must be prevented; criteria of real necessity and reasonableness must be respected; genetic modifications that could significantly alter the biodiversity and the balance of the species in the animal world must be avoided."[239]

Transplantation and personal identity

Immorality in the case of certain organs

119.   Not all organs can be donated. From the ethical perspective, the brain and the gonads are ruled out as potential transplants, inasmuch as they are connected respectively with the *personal and procreative identity of the person*. These are organs specifically connected with the uniqueness of the person, which medicine must safeguard.

Abuses in transplantation

120.   The sale of organs and the adoption of discriminatory or utilitarian criteria in selecting recipients contradict the underlying meaning of the donor's gift. As such they are morally illicit. *Abuses in transplantation* and *organ trafficking*, which often involve the most vulnerable persons, such as children, "must find the scientific and medical community ready to unite in rejecting such unacceptable practices. Therefore they are to be decisively condemned as abominable."[240]

No to organ trafficking

238   John Paul II, Address to participants in an international congress on organ transplants (August 29, 2000), n. 7: *AAS* 92 (2000), 825.

239   Pontifical Academy for Life, *Prospects for Xenotransplantation: Scientific Aspects and Ethical Considerations* (Vatican City: 2001), n. 9.

240   Benedict XVI, Address to participants in the international congress organized by the Pontifical Academy for Life (November 7, 2008): *AAS* 100 (2008), 803.

Forms of dependence

121.   Dependence, in the context of medicine and health care, is a habitual reliance on a substance or a product—such as drugs, alcohol, narcotics, or tobacco—for which the individual experiences an irrepressible need, and the deprivation of which can cause mental and physical disturbances.

Escalation of the phenomenon of dependence

The phenomenon of dependence in our societies is an increasingly worrisome and in some ways tragic reality. It is related on the one hand to the *crisis of values and meaning* from which contemporary society and culture suffer[241] and, on the other hand, to the *stress* and frustrations generated by the relentless demand for efficiency, by activism, and by the heightened competitiveness and anonymity of social interactions.

The evils caused by forms of dependence and the treatment of dependence are not the exclusive province of medicine. Medicine, however, has a preventive and therapeutic approach of its own.

Drug dependence

122.   *Drug dependence* can be an expression of the loss of meaning and of value in life, to the point of putting it at risk: many cases of death by *overdose* are true suicides, strictly speaking.

Cause of drug dependence

123.   From the moral perspective, drug abuse "is always illicit, because it implies an unjustified and irrational refusal to think, will, and act as free persons."[242] A judgment that drug use is illicit is not a judgment that condemns the

Ethical assessment of drug dependence

---

241   "At the root of alcohol and drug abuse—taking into account the painful complexity of causes and situations—there is usually an existential vacuum, due to an absence of values and a lack of self-esteem, of trust in others and in life in general" (John Paul II, Address to the participants in the Sixth International Conference on Drugs and Alcohol [November 23, 1991], n. 2: *AAS* 84 [1992], 1128).

242   Ibid., n. 4: *AAS* 84 (1992), 1130.

person, who experiences his own condition of dependence as "a heavy slavery."[243] Neither emphasizing moral guilt nor applying legal penalties can be the path to full recovery; rather, recovery must be based on the reacquisition of

Path to recovery

values, without concealing any actual moral responsibilities on the part of the drug abuser, which promote his liberation for the sake of his reintegration into family and society. This means that detoxification is more than a medical treatment: it is an integrally human intervention.[244]

Drug abuse is opposed to life

124.   Drug abuse is opposed to life. "One cannot speak of 'the freedom to take drugs' or of 'the right to drugs,' because a human being does not have the right to harm himself, and he cannot and must not ever abdicate his personal dignity, which is given to him by God,"[245] and even less does he have the right to make others pay for his choice.

Alcoholism

Ethical assessment of alcoholism

125.   Alcohol can also have harmful effects on health. In fact, excessive consumption of it tends to result in alcoholism, an expression of the dependence caused by its continuous use, and in ever higher doses. Alcohol abuse and dependence disregard the moral duty to safeguard and preserve health, and with it life. Both, in fact, produce *highly deleterious effects* for the person's physical, psychological, and spiritual health. Moreover, alcoholism can also have a social impact, inasmuch as it is frequently the cause

---

243   Cf. John Paul II, Address to the participants in the Eighth World Congress of Therapeutic Communities (September 7, 1984), n. 3: *Insegnamenti* VII/2 (1984), 347.

244   Cf. ibid., n. 7: *Insegnamenti* VII/2 (1984), 350.

245   John Paul II, Address to the participants in the Sixth International Conference on Drugs and Alcohol (November 23, 1991), n. 4: *AAS* 84 (1992), 1130. "The use of drugs inflicts very grave damage on human life and health. Their use, except on strictly therapeutic grounds, is a grave offense. Clandestine production of and trafficking in drugs are scandalous practices. They constitute direct cooperation in evil, since they encourage people to practices gravely contrary to the moral law" (*CCC*, n. 2291).

of traffic and workplace accidents; it can incite family violence and even affect a person's descendants. Alcoholism is widespread in some countries and regions, making it a true social plague. Particularly worrisome is the rise of alcohol consumption among women and youth, who start drinking at earlier ages, with destabilizing effects on their growth.[246]

126.   This *social plague* should persuade those responsible for health care activities and policies, and health care workers themselves, to promote detoxification and treatment facilities and prevention strategies, with particular attention to young people. An alcoholic is a sick person in need of medical treatment, along with help in terms of solidarity and psychotherapy. Such an individual warrants the engagement of integrally human recovery measures.

Integrally human recovery measures

Tobacco dependence

127.   By now medical research has confirmed the harmful effects of tobacco smoking on health. It harms the health of the smoker (*active smoking*) and also of those who breathe the smoke of others (*passive smoking*). Today tobacco is one of the main causes of death in the world. For this reason alone, tobacco use raises unavoidable moral questions.

Ethical assessment of tobacco dependence

Smoking is becoming more widespread among young people and among the female population. In particular, adolescents are more susceptible to dependence and to the physically and psychologically harmful effects of tobacco. Those who are responsible for health care policies and health care workers themselves cannot remain indifferent to these facts. They are charged with the work

---

246   "The economic conditions existing in society, such as high rates of poverty and unemployment, can contribute to a young person's sense of restlessness, insecurity, frustration and social alienation, and can draw that person to the fantasy world of alcohol as an escape from the problems of life" (John Paul II, Address to the participants in the Thirty-First International Institute for the Prevention and Treatment of Alcoholism [June 7, 1985]: *Insegnamenti* VIII/1 [1985], 1741).

of prevention and dissuasion, in their respective fields, through appropriate and targeted *educational activity*.

Psychotropic drugs

Prudent criteria

128.   Psychotropic drugs are a special category of pharmaceuticals designed to alleviate physical or mental sufferings in certain cases. Recourse to such psychotropic substances, when medically indicated, must adhere to very prudent criteria, so as to avoid dangerous forms of habituation and dependence.

"It is the job of health care authorities, physicians, and those responsible for research centers to work to minimize these risks by means of suitable measures of prevention and information."[247]

Ethical legitimacy

129.   Psychotropic drugs are ethically legitimate when administered for *therapeutic purposes* and with due respect for the person. The general conditions for the permissibility of any therapeutic intervention apply to them.

Respect for the patient's decision-making capacity

In particular, whenever possible, informed consent should be requested, taking into account the patient's decision-making capacity. In selecting and administering these drugs, the physician must also respect the principle of therapeutic proportionality, basing it on a careful assessment of the etiology of the symptoms and other reasons for employing these drugs.[248]

Impermissibility of nontherapeutic use and abuse

130.   The *nontherapeutic use* and the *abuse of psychotropic drugs* for the purpose of enhancing particular abilities or obtaining an artificial, euphoric serenity is morally illicit. In this way human experience is altered, falsifying the results of the subject's self-realization, putting his personal identity and authenticity at risk, and promot-

247   John Paul II, Address to the participants in the Sixth International Conference on Drugs and Alcohol (November 23, 1991), n. 4: *AAS* 84 [1992], 1130.

248   Cf. Pius XII, Address to the participants in the First International Congress of Psychopharmacology (September 9, 1958): *AAS* 50 (1958), 687–696.

ing a culture of hyperefficiency. The inappropriate use of psychotropic drugs in this way is no different from drug abuse, so the ethical judgments already formulated with regard to drug dependence apply to them as well.

Particular attention must be paid to casual recourse to psychotropic drugs in pediatric patients.

Psychology and psychotherapy

131.   It has been proved that the psychological component plays a more or less important role in all pathologies, whether as a concomitant cause or as an outcome affecting one's personal experience. *Psychosomatic medicine* addresses this and supports the therapeutic value of the personal relationship between health care worker and patient.[249]

Psychosomatic medicine

The health care worker must maintain a good relationship with the patient so that his professionalism and competence become more effective through his ability to understand the sick person. This approach, supported by an integrally human view of sickness and strengthened by faith,[250] is inscribed in such therapeutic effectiveness.

132.   Psychological disorders and illnesses can be addressed and treated with *psychotherapy*. It must be kept in mind that every form of psychotherapy has its own anthropological vision, formulates hypotheses about the origins of psychological disturbances, and proposes to the patient both its own theoretical model and a therapy that usually requires behavioral changes and, in certain cases, changes to the patient's value system. Psychotherapy can therefore affect the patient's personality and cause changes to it.

Anthropological vision of psychotherapy

---

249   Cf. Paul VI, Address to the Third World Congress of the International College of Psychosomatic Medicine (September 18, 1975): *AAS* 67 (1975), 544.

250   Cf. John Paul II, Motu Proprio *Dolentium hominum*, n. 2: *AAS* 77 (1985), 458.

The patient's state of dependence on the therapist and his hope of improvement or recovery expose him to the risk of accepting principles that conflict with his own value system. Therefore, it is necessary that the therapy be compatible with *Christian anthropology* and, where appropriate, combined with religious assistance, given that mental disturbances can have a spiritual origin as well: "The new forms of slavery to drugs and the lack of hope into which so many people fall can be explained not only in sociological and psychological terms but also in essentially spiritual terms. The emptiness in which the soul feels abandoned, despite the availability of countless therapies for body and psyche, leads to suffering. *There cannot be holistic development and universal common good unless people's spiritual and moral welfare is taken into account,* considered in their totality as body and soul."[251]

Criteria for ethical permissibility

133.   Psychotherapy is morally acceptable as a curative intervention,[252] but it must respect the patient as a person and his spiritual and religious convictions.

This respect obliges the psychotherapist to *work within the limits of the informed consent requested of and given by the patient.* "Just as it is unlawful to appropriate the goods of another or invade his corporal integrity without his permission, so it is not permissible to enter the inner world of another person against his wishes, whatever be the techniques and methods employed."[253]

The same respect obliges the therapist not to influence and force the patient's will.

Need for a high sense of ethics

134.   Most forms of psychotherapy are acceptable from the moral perspective, provided they are conducted by

251   Benedict XVI, Encyclical Letter *Caritas in veritate*, n. 76: *AAS* 101 (2009), 707.

252   "Considered in its totality, modern psychology deserves approval from the moral and religious viewpoint" (Pius XII, Address to the Thirteenth Congress of the International Association of Applied Psychology [April 10, 1958]: *AAS* 50 [1958], 274).

253   Ibid.: *AAS* 50 (1958), 276.

psychotherapists who are guided by a high sense of ethics and professionalism. Nevertheless, based on the principle of the inviolable dignity of the human person, it should be emphasized that some therapeutic methods—for example, an incorrect use of hypnosis—could be morally unacceptable if not downright dangerous for the integrity of the subject and of his family.

Pastoral care and the sacrament of the Anointing of the Sick

135.   *Pastoral care* of the sick consists in spiritual and religious assistance. It is a fundamental right of the sick person and a duty of the Church (cf. Mt 10:8; Lk 9:2). Not to provide it, to make it optional, not to promote it, or to obstruct it is to violate this right.

Right of the sick person and duty of the Church

This is an essential and specific—though not exclusive—task of health care pastoral workers. Because of the necessary interaction between the physical, psychological, and spiritual dimensions of the person and because of the duty to witness to one's own faith, every health care worker is bound to create conditions so that religious assistance is secured for whoever asks for it, whether expressly or implicitly.[254] "In Jesus, the 'Word of life,' God's eternal life is thus proclaimed and given. Thanks to this proclamation and gift, our physical and spiritual life, also in its earthly phase, acquires its full value and meaning, for

Essential and specific task of health care pastoral work

---

254 "Experience teaches that man, needing either preventive or therapeutic assistance, reveals needs that go beyond actual organic pathology. It is not only suitable treatment that he wants from the doctor—treatment which, in any case, sooner or later will inevitably prove to be insufficient—but the human support of a brother, who can share with him a life view in which even the mystery of suffering and death will make sense. And where could one find this calming response to the most important questions in life, if not in faith?" (John Paul II, Address to the World Congress of Catholic Physicians [October 3, 1982], n. 6: *Insegnamenti* V/3 [1982], 675).

God's eternal life is in fact the end to which our living in this world is directed and called."[255]

Encourage and welcome religious assistance

136.   *Religious assistance* includes the assignment or allotment of appropriate and dignified spaces for it within health care facilities, and of suitable means by which to provide it.

The health care worker must show complete willingness to encourage and welcome the sick person's request for religious assistance. Where this assistance cannot be provided by the pastoral worker for general or incidental reasons, it must be offered directly by the health care worker within possible and allowable limits, with respect to the freedom and the religious faith of the patient and in the awareness that performing this task is not a deviation from the duties of health care assistance properly speaking.

137.   Religious assistance to the sick is inscribed in the broader framework of *pastoral ministry in health care*, in other words, of the Church's presence and action aimed at bringing the Word and the grace of the Lord to suffering persons and their family members, and to the professional and volunteer workers who care for them.

Reliving God's mercy in Christ

The ministry of those priests, deacons, religious, and adequately trained lay persons who, individually or as a community, work to provide pastoral care for the sick is a reliving of the mercy of God, who in Christ bowed himself down over human suffering, and it accomplishes in a unique and privileged manner the task of evangelization, sanctification, and charity entrusted by the Lord to the Church.[256]

---

255   John Paul II, Encyclical Letter *Evangelium vitae*, n. 30: *AAS* 87 (1995), 435.

256   "From the Paschal mystery streams a singular light, a specific task that health care pastoral ministry is called to perform in the great endeavor of evangelization" (John Paul II, Address to the participants in the Second Plenary Assembly of the Pontifical Council for

This means that pastoral care of the sick has a special place in catechesis, in the liturgy, and in charitable work. Respectively, it is about giving *an evangelical meaning to sickness*, helping the patient discover the redemptive significance of suffering experienced in communion with Christ, *celebrating* the sacraments as the efficacious signs of the recreating and life-giving grace of God, and *witnessing* by *"diakonia"* (service) and *"koinonia"* (communion) to the therapeutic or healing power of charity.

Giving evangelical meaning to sickness and celebrating the sacraments

138.   In the pastoral care of the sick, God's love, which is full of truth and grace, is brought close by a special sacrament: the Anointing of the Sick.[257]

Closeness of God in the Anointing of the Sick

Administered to any Christian who is in a life-threatening condition, this sacrament is a remedy for the body and for the spirit: relief and strength for the sick person as a whole, in his corporeal-spiritual existence; a light that illuminates the mystery of suffering and death; and a hope that opens man's present up to God's future. "The whole person is made healthy, is encouraged to trust in God, and gains the strength to resist the temptations of the Evil One and avoid succumbing to anxiety about death."[258]

Specific effects of the sacraments

Like any sacrament, the Anointing of the Sick should be preceded by appropriate catechesis, so as to make the recipient aware of and responsive to the grace of the sacrament.[259]

Appropriate preparatory catechesis

Pastoral Assistance to Health Care Workers [February 11, 1992], n. 7: *AAS* 85 [1993], 264). Cf. *CCC*, n. 1503.

257   Cf. Jas 5:14–15. "People who are seriously ill have special need of the help of divine grace in what is an anxious time, lest they become dispirited, beset by temptations and prone to a diminution of their faith. This is why Christ strengthens and supports with the sacrament of anointing those who are ill" (Congregation for Divine Worship, *The Rite of Anointing and Pastoral Care of the Sick* [December 7, 1972], introduction, n. 5.) Cf. *CCC*, n. 1511.

258   Congregation for Divine Worship, *The Rite of Anointing and Pastoral Care of the Sick*, introduction, n. 6.

259   "By the grace of this sacrament the sick person receives the strength and the gift of uniting himself more closely to Christ's

Ministers of the Anointing of the Sick

139.   *Priests* (*bishops and presbyters*) *are the proper ministers of the Anointing of the Sick*,[260] who see to it that the sacrament is conferred on the faithful whose state of health is seriously threatened by old age or by grave illness or who are about to undergo major surgery.[261]

Communal celebrations of the Anointing of the Sick can serve to overcome negative prejudices and to help the faithful appreciate both the meaning of this sacrament and a sense of ecclesial solidarity.

Repetition of Anointing of the Sick

The sacrament may be repeated if the sick person, after being cured of the illness for which he received it, comes down with another, or if his condition worsens in the course of the same illness.[262]

People who can receive the Anointing of the Sick

The Anointing of the Sick may be conferred on "elderly people … if they are weak, though not dangerously ill."[263]

If the requisite conditions are present, it can also be conferred on *children* "if they are sufficiently mature to be comforted by the sacrament."[264]

In the case of patients who are *unconscious* or *do not have the use of reason, or if there is doubt about whether death has occurred yet*, the sacrament may be

---

Passion: in a certain way he is *consecrated* to bear fruit by configuration to the Savior's redemptive Passion" (*CCC*, n. 1521). "The sick who receive this sacrament, 'by freely uniting themselves to the passion and death of Christ,' 'contribute to the good of the People of God.' By celebrating this sacrament the Church, in the communion of saints, intercedes for the benefit of the sick person, and he, for his part, through this sacrament, contributes to the sanctification of the Church and to the good of all men for whom the Church suffers and offers herself through Christ to God the Father" (*CCC*, n. 1522).

260 Cf. ibid., n. 1516.

261 Cf. ibid., nn. 1514–1515.

262 Cf. ibid., n. 1515; *CIC*, can. 1004 §2.

263 Congregation for Divine Worship, *The Rite of Anointing and Pastoral Care of the Sick*, introduction, n. 11; cf. *CIC*, can. 1004 §1.

264 Ibid., n. 12; cf. *CIC*, can. 1004 §1.

administered "if they would have requested it if they had been in possession of their faculties."[265]

Ethics committees and clinical ethics counseling

140.   Concerning the organization of health care facilities, it proves advantageous to establish services that allow them to confront the bioethical challenges resulting from the continuous expansion of the increasingly sophisticated and complex possibilities of medicine, whereby the experience and sensitivity of the individual health care worker may not be enough to resolve the ethical problems encountered in practicing his profession. This role should be played by *ethics committees* and by *clinical ethics consultation* services, which ought to find a place more and more often in health care facilities.

Ethics committee and clinical ethics consultation services

In particular, ethics committees should not limit themselves to merely administrative supervision in the field of clinical experimentation, but rather should be appreciated in the area of biomedical practice, offering an opportunity to make the clinical decision-making process more reasonable and to appropriately assess the ethical values that are at stake or in conflict in everyday practice.

No to ethics committees for merely administrative supervision

Moreover clinical ethics consultation can help identify areas of conflict and ethical doubts that individual health care workers, patients, and family members may experience in clinical practice, thus facilitating their resolution by diagnostic and therapeutic decisions shared at the patient's bedside, within the framework of values proper to medicine and ethics. Similarly, ethics consultation can facilitate decision-making processes at various levels of health care policy, programming, and organization.

Facilitation of decisions through consultation

265 Congregation for Divine Worship, *The Rite of Anointing and Pastoral Care of the Sick*, introduction, n. 14; cf. *CIC*, cann. 1005, 1006.

Health care policies and the right to the preservation of health

Pertinence of the right to the preservation of health to the value of justice

141. The fundamental right to the preservation of health pertains to the *value of justice*, whereby there are no distinctions between peoples and ethnic groups, taking into account their objective living situations and stages of development, in pursuing the *common good*, which is at the same time the good of all and of each individual. Among others, the civil community in particular must take on this responsibility for the common good, including decisions in the area of health care policies. This is especially true for countries and populations at an initial or not very advanced stage of their economic development.

Fair distribution of health care facilities and financial resources

142. At the national level, therefore, a just and *fair distribution of health care facilities* must be assured, corresponding to the objective needs of the citizens. Likewise, the competent bodies at the international and global levels are called to pursue the common good with a just and fair distribution of financial resources, in keeping with the principles of *solidarity* and *subsidiarity*.

Principle of subsidiarity

In fact, subsidiarity, which is an expression of inalienable human freedom, "respects personal dignity by recognizing in the person a subject who is always capable of giving something to others. By considering reciprocity as the heart of what it is to be a human being, subsidiarity is the most effective antidote against any form of all-encompassing welfare state."[266]

Principle of solidarity

Nevertheless, "the principle of subsidiarity must remain closely linked to the principle of solidarity and vice versa, since the former without the latter gives way to social privatism, while the latter without the former gives way to paternalist social assistance that is demeaning to those in need."[267]

---

266 Benedict XVI, Encyclical Letter *Caritas in veritate*, n. 57: *AAS* 101 (2009), 692.

267 Ibid., n. 58: *AAS* 101 (2009), 693.

143.   The two principles of subsidiarity and solidarity must, in particular, be taken up and put into action both by those responsible for health care policies in the context of a fair *allocation of financial resources*, and also by those responsible for the pharmaceutical industries, especially with regard to some pathologies that have a quantitatively limited incidence, at least in the least developed countries.[268] In other words, this is about the so-called neglected diseases and rare diseases, for which both research and the possibility of a treatment depend on the solidarity of persons.

Health care policies based on the principles of subsidiarity and solidarity

According to the principles of subsidiarity and solidarity, the *international community* and *global health policies* must take responsibility for these too, inasmuch as they constitute a challenge that cannot be deferred, so that even the most vulnerable populations can satisfy the primary and fundamental good of health and its preservation.

268   The expression "least developed countries" was coined by the United Nations in 1971 to distinguish between developing countries and poorer and economically weaker countries with serious economic, institutional, and human resource problems, which are often burdened as well by geographical handicaps and by natural or manmade disasters. This expression refers, therefore, to those countries where living conditions are dramatic and there are no prospects of improvement.

DYING

144.   For the health care worker, to serve life means to respect it and care for it until its natural conclusion. Man is not the master and arbiter of life, but its faithful steward; indeed, life is a *gift from God*, and therefore it is *inviolable and non-disposable*. Neither can the health care worker consider himself an arbiter over either life or death.

Care until natural conclusion of life

145.   When clinical conditions deteriorate irreversibly, the sick person enters the terminal stage of his earthly life, and experiencing that sickness can gradually become precarious and painful. The detachment caused by the dying process may involve mental and spiritual sufferings in addition to the physical pain.

Health care workers and the terminally ill

At this stage of life, holistic and respectful care of the person must promote the *properly human and Christian dimension of dying* as the fundamental objective to be pursued. This accompaniment toward death requires compassion and professionalism on the part of psychologically and emotionally competent health care workers. Indeed, this is about human, Christian care-giving and accompaniment, to which professional and pastoral workers are called to make their qualified and dutiful contribution in accordance with their respective competencies and responsibilities.

Holistic and respectful care of the person

One's attitude toward the sick person in the terminal stage of his illness is a *test of the professionalism and ethical responsibilities of health care workers.*[269]

Test of professionalism and ethical responsibilities

---

269   "Never more than in the proximity of death and in death itself is life to be celebrated and extolled. Life must be fully respected, protected, and assisted even in one who is experiencing its natural end. ... One's attitude toward the terminally ill is often the acid test of a sense of justice and charity, of the magnanimity, responsibility and professional ability of health care workers, beginning with doctors" (John Paul II, Address to participants in an international congress of the *Omnia Hominis* Association [August 25, 1990]: *Insegnamenti* XIII/2 [1990], 328). "Such a situation can threaten the already fragile equilibrium of an individual's personal and family life, with the result that, on the one hand, the sick person, despite the help of increasingly effective medical and social assistance, risks feeling overwhelmed by his or her own frailty; and on the other hand, those close to the sick person can be moved by an

Need for
care and
assistance

146.   The *dying process* is a moment in a person's life which, although not reversible, *always deserves care and assistance*. Health care workers are called to interact with pastoral workers and family members to offer the person in the terminal stage of life the clinical, psychological, and spiritual help that will allow him, as much as humanly possible, to accept and to experience his death.

Dying among
family

When conditions permit it, and if requested directly by the patient or his relatives, the dying person must have the option of returning to his own home or to a suitable environment, thus helping him to live the final experience of his life, while assuring the necessary health care and pastoral assistance.

Palliative
care

147.   A sick person in the terminal stage of his illness should receive all forms of care that allow for alleviation of the painfulness of the dying process. These correspond to so-called *palliative care*, which together with care for his physical, psychological, and spiritual needs, tends to create a *loving presence* around the dying person and his family members.[270]

Inspiring
trust and
hope

This attentive and caring presence inspires trust and hope in the dying person and helps him to face the moment of death, and it may enable his family members to accept the death of their loved one. This is the contribution that health care and pastoral workers should offer to the dying person and his family, so that acceptance may replace denial, and *hope* may prevail over anguish.

understandable even if misplaced compassion. All this is aggravated by a cultural climate which fails to perceive any meaning or value in suffering, but rather considers suffering the epitome of evil, to be eliminated at all costs. This is especially the case in the absence of a religious outlook which could help to provide a positive understanding of the mystery of suffering" (John Paul II, Encyclical Letter *Evangelium vitae*, n. 15: *AAS* 87 [1995], 417).

270   Cf. John Paul II, Address to participants in the International Convention on Care of the Dying (March 17, 1992), n. 5: *AAS* 85 (1993), 343.

148.   At the end of his earthly existence, man is faced with a mystery: "Confronted with this mystery of death, we remain helpless; human certitudes waver. But precisely in the face of this failure, the Christian faith ... is offered as a source of serenity and peace."[271] What seems meaningless can acquire meaning.

Faith as a source of serenity and peace

For a Christian, death is not a hopeless adventure; it is the door of life that opens to eternity; it is the experience of participation in the mystery of Christ's death and resurrection.[272]

Hope of eternal life

At this decisive hour in a person's life, the witness of faith and hope of health care and pastoral workers who are caring for him can enable the dying person and his family members to glimpse God's promise of a new earth, where there will be no more death or mourning, no crying or pain, because the former things have passed away (cf. Rev 21:4 ff).

"Over and above all human comforts, no one can fail to see the enormous help given to the dying and their families by faith in God and by hope in eternal life."[273] The highest form of humanizing the dying process that health care and pastoral workers can offer is providing a faith- and hope-filled presence.

Dying with dignity

149.   In the terminal stage, the dignity of the person is elucidated in his right to die with as much serenity as possible, and with the human and Christian dignity that is owed to him.[274]

Protecting the dignity of the dying

271   Ibid., n. 2: *AAS* 85 (1993), 341. Cf. *CCC*, nn. 1006, 1009.

272   John Paul II, Encyclical Letter *Evangelium vitae*, n. 97: *AAS* 87 (1995), 512.

273   John Paul II, Address to the Pontifical Academy of Sciences (October 21, 1985), n. 6: *AAS* 78 (1986), 316.

274   Cf. Congregation for the Doctrine of the Faith, *Declaration on Euthanasia*, IV: *AAS* 72 (1980), 549.

Preserving the dignity of dying means respecting the sick person in the final stage of his life, refusing both to hasten death (euthanasia)[275] and to prolong it through *therapeutic obstinacy.*[276] Contemporary man has come to be explicitly aware of this right to be protected, at the moment of death, from "a technological attitude that threatens to become an abuse."[277] Indeed, modern medicine has means at its disposal that are capable of artificially postponing death without the patient receiving any real benefit.

*Explanation of
the principle of
proportionality
of treatment*

150.   Aware that he "is not the lord of life, ... neither is he the conqueror of death," a health care worker must choose appropriately in evaluating the means.[278] Here he applies

---

275   Whatever the reasons for it and the means employed, euthanasia consists of an action or omission which, of itself or by intention, causes death for the purpose of putting an end to suffering. It is, therefore, a form of killing which is gravely contrary to the dignity of the human person and to respect for the living God, his Creator. The error of judgment into which one may fall in good faith does not change the homicidal nature of this act, which must always be condemned and ruled out. Cf. *CCC*, n. 2276.

276   Cf. John Paul II, Encyclical Letter *Evangelium vitae*, n. 65: *AAS* 87 (1995), 475. [The Italian term "accanimento terapeutico" was used in the original *Charter for Health Care Workers* and translated as "therapeutic obstinacy." This term is used here for consistency with the original text. The concept is that of over-zealous and aggressive ("obstinate") interventions that have a genuine therapeutic aim but are not morally obligatory and may even be immoral. For English speakers, the term could cause confusion. If "obstinacy" is understood to reflect physiologically futile or extraordinary and disproportionate efforts, then the intervention of course would not be therapeutic. A helpful discussion of the terminology and its meaning in the moral tradition is found in John M. Haas, "Therapeutic Proportionality and Therapeutic Obstinacy in the Documents of the Magisterium," in *Alongside the Incurably Sick and Dying Person: Ethical and Practical Aspects*, Proceedings of the Fourteenth Assembly of the Pontifical Academy for Life, 25–27 February 2008, ed. Elio Sgreccia and Jean Laffitte (Vatican City: Libreria Editrice Vaticana, 2009), 143–157.—TRANS.]

277   Congregation for the Doctrine of the Faith, *Declaration on Euthanasia*, IV: *AAS* 72 (1980), 549.

278   Cf. John Paul II, Address to the Pontifical Academy of Sciences (October 21, 1985), n. 5: *AAS* 78 (1986), 315.

the principle—discussed earlier—of the *proportionality of treatment*, which can be defined as follows: "When inevitable death is imminent in spite of the means used, it is permitted in conscience to take the decision to refuse forms of treatment that would only secure a precarious and burdensome prolongation of life, so long as the normal care due to the sick person in similar cases is not interrupted."[279] Therefore the physician has no reason to torment himself as though he had not provided any assistance.

Forgoing these treatments, which would only procure a tenuous and painful prolongation of life, can also indicate respect for the dying person's will, expressed in *statements or advance directives* concerning treatment, while excluding any act of euthanasia.

Forgoing treatment and the dying person's will

The patient may express in advance his will concerning the treatments to which he would or would not wish to be subjected in a case where, over the course of his sickness or because of unexpected trauma, he is no longer capable of expressing his own consent or disagreement. "The decisions should be made by the patient if he is competent and able or, if not, by those legally entitled to act for the patient whose reasonable will and legitimate interests must always be respected."[280]

The physician is not a mere executor, however; he keeps the right and the duty not to carry out wishes that conflict with his own conscience.

Civil laws and conscientious objection

151.   No health care worker, therefore, can become the defender of a non-existing right, even if euthanasia were requested by the subject in question when he was fully conscious. Moreover, "any State which made such a request legitimate and authorized it to be carried out

---

279 Congregation for the Doctrine of the Faith, *Declaration on Euthanasia*, IV: *AAS* 72 (1980), 551. Cf. John Paul II, Encyclical Letter *Evangelium vitae*, n. 65: *AAS* 87 (1995), 475.

280 *CCC*, n. 2278.

would be legalizing a case of suicide-murder, contrary to the fundamental principles of absolute respect for life and of the protection of every innocent life."[281] Laws to this effect would be "radically opposed not only to the good of the individual but also to the common good; as such they are completely lacking in authentic juridical validity."[282] Similar laws cease to be true civil law that obliges in conscience;[283] "instead there is a grave and clear obligation to oppose them by conscientious objection."[284]

Impermissibility of all types of formal cooperation in evil actions

In this regard, the general principles about *cooperation in evil actions* are restated as follows: "Christians, like all people of good will, are called upon under grave obligation of conscience not to cooperate formally in practices which, even if permitted by civil legislation, are contrary to God's law. Indeed, from the moral standpoint, it is never licit to cooperate formally in evil. Such cooperation occurs when an action, either by its very nature or by the form it takes in a concrete situation, can be defined as a direct participation in an act against innocent human life or a sharing in the immoral intention of the person committing it. This cooperation can never be justified either by invoking respect for the freedom of others or by appealing to the fact that civil law permits it or requires it. Each individual in fact has moral responsibility for the acts which he personally performs; no one can be exempted from this responsibility, and on the basis of it everyone will be judged by God himself (cf. Rom 2:6; 14:12)."[285]

---

281 John Paul II, Encyclical Letter *Evangelium vitae*, n. 72: *AAS* 87 (1995), 485.

282 Ibid.

283 Cf. ibid.

284 Ibid., n. 73: *AAS* 87 (1995), 486. Cf. ibid., n. 74: *AAS* 87 (1995), 487–488; Benedict XVI, Address to the participants in the Thirteenth General Assembly of the Pontifical Academy for Life (February 24, 2007): *AAS* 99 (2007), 283–87.

285 John Paul II, Encyclical Letter *Evangelium vitae*, n. 74: *AAS* 87 (1995), 487. In a similar context, precise duties are required of Catholics who are involved in politics, particularly in developing

Nutrition and hydration

152.   *Nutrition* and *hydration*, even if administered artificially, are classified as basic care owed to the dying person
when they do not prove to be too burdensome or without
any benefit. The unjustified discontinuation thereof can be
tantamount to a real act of euthanasia: "The administration
of food and water even by artificial means is, in principle,
an ordinary and proportionate means of preserving life.
It is therefore obligatory to the extent to which, and for
as long as, it is shown to accomplish its proper finality,
which is the hydration and nourishment of the patient. In
this way suffering and death by starvation and dehydration
are prevented."[286]

Nutrition and hydration are obligatory in principle

The use of analgesics in the terminal stage

153.   Pain management is to be included among the
types of care administered to a person in the terminal stage
of life.

Permissibility of the use of analgesics for sick persons in the terminal stages of life

Pain in the final moments of life can take on a spiritual significance for a sick person and, in particular for a
Christian, can be accepted as "participation in the passion"
and "union with the redemptive sacrifice of Christ" (cf.
Col 1:24). One may therefore refuse the administration of
analgesic treatments for these reasons.[287]

---

and approving laws that limit or abrogate the evil only partially;
cf. ibid., n. 73: *AAS* 87 (1995), 486–487.

286   Congregation for the Doctrine of the Faith, *Responses to Certain
Questions of the United States Conference of Catholic Bishops
concerning Artificial Nutrition and Hydration* (August 1, 2007):
AAS 99 (2007), 820.

287   A Christian may freely accept pain without alleviating or mitigat-
ing it by the use of painkillers: Congregation for the Doctrine of the
Faith, *Declaration on Euthanasia*, III: *AAS* 72 (1980), 547. "The
Redeemer suffered in place of man and for man. Every man has
his own share in the Redemption. Each one is also called to share
in that suffering through which the Redemption was accomplished.
He is called to share in that suffering through which all human suffering has also been redeemed. In bringing about the Redemption

This is not a general norm, however. Indeed, heroic behavior cannot be demanded of everyone.[288] In fact, pain can often diminish a person's physical and moral strength.[289]

Proper human and Christian care allows the use of drugs that are designed to alleviate or eliminate pain as necessary in treatment, with the patient's consent, even though they may result in torpor or diminished lucidity.

Risk of hastening death

154.   In the terminal stage, high doses of analgesics may sometimes be necessary to alleviate pain; this entails the risk of collateral effects and complications, including the *hastening of death*. It is necessary, therefore, that analgesics be prescribed prudently and *according to the standards of the art*. "The use of painkillers to alleviate the sufferings of the dying, even at the risk of shortening their days, can be morally in conformity with human dignity if death is not willed as either an end or a means, but only foreseen and tolerated as inevitable."[290] In this case "death is in no way intended or sought, even if the risk of it is reasonably taken; the intention is simply to relieve pain

through suffering, Christ has also raised human suffering to the level of the Redemption. Thus each man, in his suffering, can also become a sharer in the redemptive suffering of Christ" (John Paul II, Apostolic Letter *Salvifici doloris*, n. 19: *AAS* 76 [1984], 226).

288   Pius XII, Address to an international assembly of physicians and surgeons (February 24, 1957): *AAS* 49 (1957), 147; Pius XII, Address to the participants in the First International Congress of Psychopharmacology (September 9, 1958): *AAS* 50 (1958), 687–696.

289   Sufferings "aggravate the state of weakness and physical exhaustion, impeding the impulse of the spirit and debilitating the moral powers instead of supporting them. The suppression of pain, instead, brings physical and mental relief, making prayer easier and enabling one to give oneself more generously" (Pius XII, Address to an international assembly of physicians and surgeons (February 24, 1957): *AAS* 49 [1957], 144).

290   *CCC*, n. 2279; cf. Pius XII, Address to the participants in the First International Congress of Psychopharmacology (September 9, 1958): *AAS* 50 (1958), 694.

effectively, using for this purpose painkillers available to medicine."[291]

155.   Moreover, there is the possibility of painkillers and narcotics causing a *loss of consciousness* in the dying person. Such usage deserves particular consideration.[292]

In the presence of unbearable pain that is resistant to typical pain-management therapies, if the moment of death is near or if there are good reasons for anticipating a particular crisis at the moment of death, a serious clinical indication can involve, with the sick person's consent, the administration of drugs that cause a loss of consciousness.

Criteria for deep palliative sedation

This deep palliative sedation in the terminal stage, when clinically motivated, can be morally acceptable provided that it is done with the patient's consent, that appropriate information is given to the family members, that any intention of euthanasia is ruled out, and that the patient has been able to perform his moral, familial, and religious duties: "As they approach death people ought to be able to satisfy their moral and family duties, and above all they ought to be able to prepare in a fully conscious way for their definitive meeting with God."[293] Therefore, "it is not right to deprive the dying person of consciousness without a serious reason."[294]

291   Congregation for the Doctrine of the Faith, *Declaration on Euthanasia*, III: *AAS* 72 (1980), 548. Cf. Pius XII, Address to an international assembly of physicians and surgeons (February 24, 1957): *AAS* 49 (1957), 146; Pius XII, Address to the participants in the First International Congress of Psychopharmacology (September 9, 1958): *AAS* 50 (1958), 697–698. Cf. John Paul II, Encyclical Letter *Evangelium vitae*, n. 65: *AAS* 87 (1995), 475–476.

292   Cf. Congregation for the Doctrine of the Faith, *Declaration on Euthanasia*, III: *AAS* 72 (1980), 548.

293   John Paul II, Encyclical Letter *Evangelium vitae*, n. 65: *AAS* 87 (1995), 476; Congregation for the Doctrine of the Faith, *Declaration on Euthanasia*, III: *AAS* 72 (1980), 548.

294   John Paul II, Encyclical Letter *Evangelium vitae*, n. 65: *AAS* 87 (1995), 476; cf. Pius XII, Address to an international assembly of physicians and surgeons (February 24, 1957): *AAS* 49 (1957), 138–143.

Palliative sedation in the stages closest to the moment of death must be induced according to correct ethical protocols and subjected to continuous monitoring, and it must not involve the discontinuation of basic care.

Telling the truth to the dying person

Duty to communicate

156.   A person has the right to be informed about his own state of health. This right does not lapse even in the case of an unfavorable diagnosis and prognosis, and it implies that the physician has a duty to respectfully communicate the patient's conditions.

The prospect of death makes this notification difficult and dramatic, but this does not exempt the physician from *truthfulness*. Communication between the dying person and his caretakers cannot be established in fiction. This is never a humane option for the dying person, and it does nothing to help make dying more human.

Responsibility to fulfill certain duties

There are *important responsibilities associated with this information that cannot be delegated.* Death's approach brings with it the responsibility of fulfilling certain duties concerning family relations, the settlement of any professional matters, and the resolution of outstanding debts or other obligations to third parties. Therefore, a person should never be left in ignorance about his own real clinical conditions in the decisive hour of his life.

Discernment and human tact

157.   The duty of telling a patient the truth in the terminal stage requires the *discernment and tact* of health care personnel.

Relationship of trust in love and charity

It cannot consist of distant and indifferent communication. The truth must not be withheld, but neither must it be simply announced: it must be communicated in love and charity. This is a matter of establishing with the patient a relationship of trust, welcome, and dialogue that is able to find the right moments and words. It is a way of talking that is able to discern and respect the timing the patient needs and to follow it. It is a way of speaking that is able to take his questions and also to elicit them, so as to direct him gradually toward knowledge of the status of his life and health. Someone who seeks to be present to the patient and sensitive to his fate will be able to find the words and the answers that allow him to communicate in truth and in charity (cf. Eph 4:15).

158. "Every single case has its demands, depending on the sensitivity and the abilities of each one, on relations with the patient and on his status; foreseeing his possible reactions (rebellion, depression, resignation, etc.), one will prepare to confront them calmly and tactfully."[295] The important thing is not just the accuracy of what is said, but the *relation of solidarity* with the sick person. It is not merely a matter of transmitting clinical facts, but of communicating significant truths.

Relationship of solidarity with the sick person

In such a relationship, the prospect of death does not appear inevitable and loses its distressing power: the patient does not feel abandoned and condemned to death. The truth communicated to him in this way does not shut him off from hope, because it can make him feel alive in a *relationship of sharing and communion*. He is not alone with his illness: he feels truly understood, at peace with himself and with others. He is himself as a person. His life, despite everything, has meaning, and it unfolds within a horizon of real meaning that transcends the dying process.

Relationship of sharing and communion

Religious care of the dying person

159. The *spiritual crisis* evoked as death draws near prompts the Church to become for the dying person and his family the bearer of the light of hope, which only faith can shine on the mystery of death. Death is an event that introduces one into God's life, about which only revelation can pronounce a word of truth. The proclamation of the Gospel, which is "full of grace and truth" (Jn 1:14),

Proclaiming the Gospel in the face of death

---

295 John Paul II, Address to participants in an international congress of the *Omnia Hominis* Association (August 25, 1990): *Insegnamenti* XIII/2 (1990), 328.

accompanies the Christian from the beginning to the end of life—which conquers death—and opens human dying to the greatest hope.

Forms of evangelization

160.   It is therefore necessary to give an *evangelical meaning to death*: proclaiming the Gospel to the dying person. This is a pastoral duty of the ecclesial community in all its members, according to each one's responsibilities. A particular task belongs to the health care chaplain, who is called in a singular way to provide pastoral care for the dying within the broader scope of his care for the sick.

For him this task involves not only the personal role at the bedside of the dying persons entrusted to his care, but also the promotion of this pastoral work in terms of the organization of religious services, training and sensitizing health care workers and volunteers, as well as involving relatives and friends. The expressive forms of the proclamation of the Gospel to the dying person are charity, prayer, and the sacraments.

Love for God in our neighbor

161.   *Charity* means the giving, welcoming presence that establishes with the dying person a communion made up of attention, understanding, thoughtfulness, patience, sharing, and giving.

Charity sees in him, in a unique way, the face of the suffering and dying Christ who calls us to love. Charity toward the dying person is a privileged expression of love for God in our neighbor (cf. Mt 25:31–40). To love him with Christian charity is to help him recognize God's mysterious presence at his side and to make him experience it vividly: the Father's love shines through the brother's charity.

Communion with God in the communion of saints

162.   Charity opens the dying person's relation to *prayer*, in other words, to communion with God. In it he relates to God as Father, who welcomes the children who return to Him.

To encourage prayer in the dying person and to pray with him is to reveal the horizons of divine life to him. At the same time, it is to enter into that communion of saints in which all the relationships that death seems to break off irremediably are reestablished in a new way.

163.   A privileged moment of prayer with the terminally ill person is the celebration of the *sacraments*: being signs of God's saving presence, "Penance, the Anointing of the Sick, and the Eucharist as viaticum constitute at the end of Christian life 'the sacraments that prepare for our heavenly homeland' or the sacraments that complete the earthly pilgrimage."[296]

Salvific sacramental presence of Christ

In particular, in the sacrament of *Reconciliation* or *Penance*, the dying person, at peace with God, is at peace with himself and with his neighbor.

"In addition to the Anointing of the Sick, the Church offers those who are about to leave this life the Eucharist as viaticum." Received at this moment of passage, the Eucharist, as viaticum, is the sacrament of "passing over" from death to life, from this world to the Father, and it gives the dying person the strength to confront the final, decisive stage of his journey in life.[297] It follows that it is important for the Christian to request it, and it is also a duty of the Church to administer it.[298] The minister of viaticum is the priest. If no priest is available, it may be conferred by the deacon or, in his absence, by an extraordinary minister of the Eucharist.[299]

164.   In this faith which is full of charity, human powerlessness before the mystery of death is not experienced as distressing and paralyzing. A Christian can find hope, and in it the possibility, despite everything, of living out rather than being merely subjected to death.

Faith full of charity

---

296   *CCC*, n. 1525.

297   Cf. ibid., n. 1524.

298   "All baptized Christians who can receive communion are obliged to receive viaticum, if in danger of death from any cause. Pastors must ensure that the administration of this sacrament is not delayed, but that it is made available to the faithful while they are still in possession of their faculties" (Congregation for Divine Worship, *The Rite of Anointing and Pastoral Care of the Sick*, introduction, n. 27).

299   Cf. ibid., n. 29.

Destroying life

Inviolable
right to life

165.   The *inviolability of human life* means and implies, ultimately, the unlawfulness of any act directly aimed at destroying it. "The inviolability of the innocent human being's right to life 'from the moment of conception until death' is a sign and requirement of the very inviolability of the person to whom the Creator has given the gift of life."[300]

God's
exclusive
right

166.   This is why "no one can make an attempt on the life of an innocent person without opposing God's love for that person, without violating a fundamental right."[301]

Categorical
no to
any other
authority

Man receives this right *immediately from God* (not from others: parents, society, or any human authority). "Therefore, there is no man, no human authority, no science, no 'indication' at all—whether it be medical, eugenic, social, economic, or moral—that may offer or give a valid judicial title for a *direct* deliberate disposal of an innocent human life, that is, a disposal which aims at its destruction, whether as an end in itself or as a means to achieve the end, perhaps in no way at all illicit."[302]

In particular, "nothing and no one can in any way permit the killing of an innocent human being, whether a fetus or an embryo, an infant or an adult, an old person, or

---

300   Congregation for the Doctrine of the Faith, Instruction *Donum vitae*, n. 4: *AAS* 80 (1988), 75–76. Cf. John Paul II, Address to participants in the "Movement for Life" (October 29, 1985), n. 2: *Insegnamenti* VIII/2 (1985), 933–936.

301   Congregation for the Doctrine of the Faith, *Declaration on Euthanasia*, I: *AAS* 72 (1980), 544. Cf. John Paul II, Encyclical Letter *Veritatis splendor*, n. 13: *AAS* 85 (1993), 1143.

302   Pius XII, Discourse to the Italian Catholic Union of Midwives (October 29, 1951): *AAS* 43 (1951), 838. "Scripture specifies the prohibition contained in the fifth commandment: 'Do not slay the innocent and the righteous.' The deliberate murder of an innocent person is gravely contrary to the dignity of the human being, to the golden rule, and to the holiness of the Creator. The law forbidding it is universally valid: it obliges each and everyone, always and everywhere" (*CCC*, n. 2261).

one suffering from an incurable disease, or a person who is dying. Furthermore, no one is permitted to ask for this act of killing, either for himself or herself or for another person entrusted to his or her care, nor can he or she consent to it, either explicitly or implicitly. Nor can any authority legitimately recommend or permit such an action. For it is a question of the violation of the divine law, an offense against the dignity of the human person, a crime against life, and an attack on humanity."[303]

167.   As "ministers of life and never agents of death,"[304] it is up to health care workers "to safeguard life, to be watchful over its evolution and development throughout its whole existence, respecting the plan drawn up by the Creator."[305]

Duty to safeguard life

    This vigilant ministry of safeguarding human life rejects *homicide* as a morally grave act that contradicts the medical mission, and it opposes voluntary death, *suicide*, as "unacceptable," by dissuading anyone who might attempt it.[306]

Particular vigilance

303 Congregation for the Doctrine of the Faith, *Declaration on Euthanasia*, II: *AAS* 72 (1980), 546. "Any discrimination based on the various stages of life is no more justified than any other discrimination. The right to life remains complete in an old person, even one greatly weakened; it is not lost by one who is incurably sick. The right to life is no less to be respected in the small infant just born than in the mature person" (CDF, *Declaration on Procured Abortion* [June 18, 1974], n. 12: *AAS* 66 [1974], 737–738).

304 John Paul II, Address to the Association of Italian Catholic Physicians (December 28, 1978): *Insegnamenti* I (1978), 438.

305 John Paul II, Address to the World Congress of Catholic Physicians (October 3, 1982): *Insegnamenti* V/3 (1982), 671.

306 Congregation for the Doctrine of the Faith, *Declaration on Euthanasia*, I: *AAS* 72 (1980), 545. "Everyone has the duty to lead his or her life in accordance with God's plan. ... Intentionally causing one's own death, or suicide ... on the part of a person is to be considered as a rejection of God's sovereignty and loving plan. Furthermore, suicide is also often a refusal of love for self, the denial of a natural instinct to live, a flight from the duties of justice and charity owed to one's neighbor, to various communities or to the whole of society—although, as is generally recognized, at times there are psychological factors present that can diminish

Among the methods of destroying life by homicide or suicide, there are two—abortion and euthanasia—about which this ministry today must be particularly vigilant and in a certain way prophetic, because of the cultural and legislative context, which is very often insensitive, if not outright favorable, to their spread.

Euthanasia

No to euthanasia and the euthanasia mentality

168.   The pity aroused by the pain and suffering of terminally ill patients, children with disabilities, the mentally ill, and the elderly can be the context in which the temptation to commit euthanasia becomes increasingly strong—in other words, to take control of death, causing it in advance and thus "gently" putting an end to one's own life or that of someone else.[307]

"Euthanasia in the strict sense is understood to be an action or omission which of itself and by intention causes death, with the purpose of eliminating all suffering. 'Euthanasia's terms of reference, therefore, are to be found in the intention of the will and in the methods used.'"[308]

In reality, what might seem logical and humane proves to be absurd and inhumane when examined more closely. We are looking at one of the most alarming symptoms of the culture of death which, especially in more highly developed societies, makes the cost of care that disabled and infirm persons require appear to be too burdensome and intolerable. This is because these societies are organized "almost exclusively on the basis of criteria of productive efficiency, according to which a

responsibility or even completely remove it. However, one must clearly distinguish suicide from that sacrifice of one's life whereby for a higher cause, such as God's glory, the salvation of souls or the service of one's brethren, a person offers his or her own life or puts it in danger " (ibid.).

307   Cf. John Paul II, Encyclical Letter *Evangelium vitae*, n. 64: *AAS* 87 (1995), 475.

308   Ibid., n. 65: *AAS* 87 (1995), 475.

hopelessly impaired life no longer has any value."[309] But everyone who is "sincerely open to truth and goodness can, by the light of reason and the hidden action of grace, come to recognize in the natural law written in the heart (cf. Rom 2:14–15) the sacred value of human life from its very beginning until its end, and can affirm the right of every human being to have this primary good respected to the highest degree."[310] *Euthanasia, therefore, is a homicidal act, which no end can justify.*[311]

No to the alleged right to euthanasia

169.   The medical personnel and other health care workers—faithful to their task of "always being at the service of life and assisting it to the end"[312]—cannot lend themselves to any act of euthanasia, not even at the request of the interested party, much less of his relatives. Indeed, *there is no right to dispose arbitrarily of one's own life,* and for this reason no health care worker can become the executor of a nonexistent right.

Loving care and presence

170.   "The pleas of gravely ill people who sometimes ask for death are not to be understood as implying a true desire for euthanasia; in fact, it is almost always a case of an anguished plea for help and love. What a sick person needs, besides medical care, is love, the human and supernatural warmth with which the sick person can and ought to be surrounded by all those close to him or her, parents and children, doctors and nurses."[313]

Medicine is for life

The patient who finds himself surrounded by a loving human and Christian presence does not fall into

309   Cf. ibid., n. 64: *AAS* 87 (1995), 474.

310   Ibid., n. 2: *AAS* 87 (1995), 402.

311   Cf. ibid., n. 65: *AAS* 87 (1995), 477.

312   Paul VI, Address to the Third World Congress of the International College of Psychosomatic Medicine (September 18, 1975): *AAS* 67 (1975), 545.

313   Congregation for the Doctrine of the Faith, *Declaration on Euthanasia,* II: *AAS* 72 (1980), 546; John Paul II, Address to participants in the International Convention on Care of the Dying (March 17, 1992), nn. 3, 5: *AAS* 85 (1993), 341–343.

the depression and anguish of those who, in contrast, feel abandoned to their destiny of suffering and death, and ask to put an end to it. This is why *euthanasia is a defeat* for anyone who theoretically defends it, decides on it, and carries it out.

171. Euthanasia is a crime in which health care workers, who are always and only guardians of life, can in no way cooperate.[314]

At the service of human life

For medical science it marks "a backward step of surrender, as well as an insult to the personal dignity of the one who is dying."[315] Its increasing acceptance as a further foothold of the culture of death after abortion must be understood as a dramatic call to efficacious and unconditional fidelity toward life.

314 John Paul II, Address to the Pontifical Academy of Sciences (October 21, 1985), n. 3: *AAS* 78 (1986), 314.

315 John Paul II, Address to participants in a course on human preleukemias (November 15, 1985), n. 5: *AAS* 78 (1986), 361.

CONCLUSION

Fidelity to life, which is a gift from God, in its end as in its beginning, in its flourishing and in its decline, is an obligation for every man and every woman of good will, but without doubt "a unique responsibility belongs to health care personnel: doctors, pharmacists, nurses, chaplains, men and women religious, administrators, and volunteers. Their profession calls for them to be guardians and servants of human life. In today's cultural and social context, in which science and the practice of medicine risk losing sight of their inherent ethical dimension, health care professionals can be strongly tempted at times to become manipulators of life, or even agents of death. In the face of this temptation, their responsibility today is greatly increased. Its deepest inspiration and strongest support lie in the intrinsic and undeniable ethical dimension of the health care profession, something already recognized by the ancient and still relevant Hippocratic Oath, which requires every doctor to commit himself to absolute respect for human life and its sacredness."[316]

Intrinsic and undeniable ethical dimension of the health care profession

God, who loves life, has entrusted it to the hands of man so that he might be its impassioned guardian. In order to respond to this ennobling vocation, it is necessary to have the willingness to undergo an interior conversion, to purify one's heart, and to find a new outlook. "It is the outlook of those who see life in its deeper meaning, who grasp its utter gratuitousness, its beauty and its invitation to freedom and responsibility. It is the outlook of those who do not presume to take possession of reality but instead accept it as a gift, discovering in all things the reflection of the Creator and seeing in every person his living image (cf. Gen 1:27; Ps 8:5). This outlook does not give in to discouragement when confronted by those who are sick, suffering, outcast, or at death's door. Instead, in all these situations it feels challenged to find meaning, and

Need for an interior conversion

---

316   John Paul II, Encyclical Letter *Evangelium vitae*, n. 89: *AAS* 87 (1995), 502.

precisely in these circumstances it is open to perceiving in the face of every person a call to encounter, dialogue, and solidarity. It is time for all of us to adopt this outlook, and with deep religious awe to rediscover the ability to revere and honor every person."[317]

317   Ibid., n. 83: *AAS* 87 (1995), 495.

INDEX

INDEX

References are to paragraph numbers.